THE SEVENTH DAY

Kris Doulos

authorHOUSE®

AuthorHouse™
1663 Liberty Drive
Bloomington, IN 47403
www.authorhouse.com
Phone: 1 (800) 839-8640

Published by AuthorHouse   04/13/2017

ISBN: 978-1-5246-8696-3 (sc)
ISBN: 978-1-5246-8695-6 (e)

Library of Congress Control Number: 2017905284

CONTENTS

INTRODUCTION

What humans must have for an orderly life is their most destructive enemy. This is a presentation of factual information based upon biblical and other historical information. It relates to the history of man and why there is so much conflict which ends in death. The author is not a religious person. He presents the information in the Bible as a researcher collecting legitimate information, essential for full and accurate knowledge of man and his world. This writing will show how people with knowledge of good and evil have consistently destroyed themselves because of their preference for knowledge that produces evil results.

In addition to the information in the Old Testament part of the Bible, Peter, along with eleven other men, spent about 3 ½ years learning information from Christ. Christ said many things that confused the people, including the apostles. By using physical things as parallels of nonphysical things and events, Christ tried to give man a view beyond that of his world; a view which is not seen with physical eyes. This is difficult because the human brain, which processes information, is physical and has difficulty understanding even with a comparison of physical and nonphysical things.

The physical world and its functions are a parallel of the nonphysical world. An ability to understand the nonphysical world is increased by using things seen in the physical world of time as a parallel to things not seen in the nonphysical, timeless world. For instance, to understand God, a person looks at the good qualities inside himself because he is a god living in a human body who is a duplicate of God.

Since time does not exist in the nonphysical realm, a thousand years or one day is the same in the timeless realm. According to Peter, this is what Christ said. **According to the Lord, one day**

is the same as one thousand years and one thousand years is the same as one day. (2 Peter 3:8). This writing is based upon the assumption what Christ said is a clue to comparing the seven original days with the seven millennial days. The seventh millennial day has just begun at the time of this writing. Numbers have a double meaning. They represent a quantity and they also represent an idea. In this writing numbers are used to assist in identifying the meanings and parallels of an original day and a millennial day. Assigning a meaning to a number is known as "Gematria".

While the Law of Gematria is not mentioned by name in the Bible, the Apocalypse (Revelation) cannot be understood without the use of Gematria. There is evidence the events of each of the seven days of creation are not only parallels to events in the millennial days; the numbers represent a common meaning for both. In comparing the events of one day with the events of one thousand years, something that happened in the one day must represent one or more things that were the highlights of the one thousand years. This writing is a condensed history of God and man from the beginning of time to the present time. The ages of people recorded in the Bible is accepted as the correct time that has passed since creation. This is a focus upon the difference in the destructive force of knowledge and the life-giving, creative force of faith.

Knowledge exerts a powerful magnetic force upon the human brain. The following story illustrates what happens to people who blindly pursue knowledge while ignoring evidence of its destructive force. A group of young men were camping on an island in the Mississippi River. That night they were sitting around a fire on a beach. The night was dark except for the light of a crescent moon and the fire. A young man sitting near the fire watched as flying insects landed on the sand near the fire and began crawling toward it. Before they could reach the flames the heat would kill them. The distance from the fire where the insects collapsed and died was from about eight to sixteen inches. Newcomers would crawl over the dead bodies of other insects in their effort to get to the fire. None ever made it. It seemed they were so focused on the fire they ignored the heat and pile of dead bodies over which they were crawling. This strange activity continued as long as the fire was burning.

Later in life this young man could still visualize the sight of the insects crawling over dead bodies to get to the fire. He realized what he saw on the island with the insects is what happens to most of the human race. The insects were crawling toward the fire while ignoring the dead bodies over which they were crawling. In the same way humans pursue knowledge while ignoring the dead bodies destroyed by knowledge. Just as the insects did not understand the fire could give them light and warmth but also kill them; many people do not understand knowledge can do the same. Since Adam chose knowledge instead of the words of God, man has been forced to rely upon the knowledge in his brain to guide him through life. Some of that knowledge produces good results but, by observing civilization through the centuries, it is obvious, most of the results are evil.

There are many religious beliefs in the world but the three that have similar teachings about God are Jews, Muslims and Christians. The knowledge of each tells them God approves them over the others and all other people in this world. They are so committed to the light of their knowledge; they depend upon it to reach God. Like the insects; instead of enjoying the good knowledge provides; they pursue knowledge until it replaces God.

When Adam ignored the warning given him by God and ate the fruit of the tree of knowledge of good and evil, he became infected with the same kind of ignorance that caused the insects to kill themselves trying the reach the flames. From that time on, whatever good knowledge he had was challenged by the magnetic force of evil knowledge. Because knowledge provides skill, wealth and power, it has a powerful magnetic force. The force which seeks to satisfy the desires of the body and its brain gives the knowledge of evil a great advantage.

People use different standards with which they arrive at what they believe is truth. Truth is good knowledge. This leaves the impression there are many truths even though one may contradict another. Pilate asked Christ, "What is truth?" Christ demonstrated his knowledge of truth with the many supernatural things he did. Truth reveals reality and what to do to change what is wrong into what is right. Truth enables a human to be like God.

Here are other reasons used by people to decide if something is true; 1. Personal experience: 2. People who think the way they think: 3. People in schools of learning who present information they like or don't have sufficient information to contradict: 4 Ancient records of the history of something or someone: 5. Interpretations of documents like the Torah, Quran and words of Christ: 6. Traditions produced by interpretations and rituals: 7. Words of trusted leaders, like Moses, Christ and Muhammad: 8. a combination of one or more of these reasons. All of these can provide confidence for a human brain but knowledge is as vast as God. Only a tiny bit can be known by any human. A person who thinks he can successfully walk the path of life with such a tiny bit of knowledge is foolish. Something else is required.

The more a person learns, the more he is able to realize how much he hasn't learned. Knowledge is like a tiny circle on a huge surface. The diameter represents what a person knows and the perimeter touches the vastness of what he doesn't know. As he learns, both the diameter and perimeter enlarge, causing him to see how much more he doesn't know. A person whose confidence is in what he knows, without respect for what he doesn't know, may not realize how much of what he doesn't know affects what he knows. The brain uses knowledge in its effort to understand God and this world. The god living in a human body uses faith to understand God and this world. The brain is limited to seeing the knowledge inside the circle. Faith can produce an awareness of what is outside the circle.

God designed humans with the ability to distinguish between a truth and a lie. The god residing inside the body, screens incoming information. A person not biased by a like or dislike of the information, can be guided by truth. A polygraph can usually detect changes in the body when a person is lying. This is the effect the god, living in the body, has on the body when the brain decides to lie. A lie is a path to ignorance that is tangent to the path of truth. The more a person lies the farther he moves away from the path of truth and the more ignorant he becomes. Logic and truth cease to be guides for his beliefs and decisions. Truth is reality; truth is "what is". A lie doesn't change "what is"; it only exposes a person's attitude to reject "what is".

Before Adam disobeyed God he was like a person standing in an open place looking at unlimited knowledge. After he disobeyed God he was like an invalid confined to his bed inside his house with his brain spoon-feeding him. A wise person looks at the knowledge inside his circle and then trusts God for the knowledge outside his circle. When Adam chose knowledge instead of God, he set a precedent for all mankind to make decisions based upon what is inside the circle instead of trusting God who knows all the information outside the circle. Trusting God permits a person to enjoy the light and warmth of knowledge without being consumed by it.

Often, truth appears to be criticism. It is criticism only when it is spoken with a hostile or judgmental attitude. When Christ spoke truth, people desiring to protect what they had learned from other sources, became emotional and hostile. They tried to protect their knowledge inside their circle of knowledge instead of fairly evaluating information coming from outside their circle of knowledge. A lover of truth may not accept certain information but he doesn't try to destroy the messenger of the information.

Christ reminded the Jewish leaders who were reacting to what he said; it would not be him but his words that would judge them. He also told them they could not serve God and what they believed. Mammon (KJV) is a transliteration. If translated, it represents the object of a person's confidence or faith. Because what God tells a person may be different from what he has learned, a closed minded person may not respond to God. When this is true, he cannot obey both, God and what he believes. A wise person listens to all incoming information without emotionally defending his existing information. Truth does not need defending.

Before Adam sinned, all knowledge was good so, without a conflict, there was no need for a choice. Whatever God said he did. The fruit of the tree of knowledge was a mixture of good and evil knowledge. This caused conflict in his brain and prevented it having a single thought which is necessary for faith. This inability to have faith is what separated him from God. It does the same with people. Trust doesn't require a choice; it accepts instructions given because of the one giving them. Instead of operating with the intelligence of God, Adam would now be forced to operate with the winner of the good and evil knowledge in his brain. God's voice is not a memory of something learned or a reasoning of the brain using knowledge. Each time God speaks to a god in a body, that god is placed in the same position as Adam and Eve; he must trust what God tells him or choose between the mixed knowledge in his brain.

Because knowledge is different in different people, there is no way complete agreement can be reached without compromise. Just as different people disagree, the two parts of a person disagrees. This makes it extremely difficult for a person to have inner agreement which is necessary for faith. Even people deeply devoted to each other and to God will not always reach agreement with self or with each other. In the absence of faith, knowledge is used to establish certain rules and guidelines so thinking and conduct can be regulated by these rules, accepted by most of the people in a group. This reduces conflict.

A person has some knowledge that is good and some that is evil. The statement, "there is good in everyone", is true because each person has a mixture of good and evil knowledge even though one might greatly outweigh the other. The body has desires designed into it that have no concept of good and evil. Because the brain is physical like the body, its concept of what is good and evil is based upon the information it contains. Its opinions and decisions are biased toward satisfying itself and its body. It is similar to a parent letting a child have his way even if it is harmful to the child. Like that parent, the brain will make decisions to please the body even if the decisions are harmful for the body.

The source of good information is God who speaks to the god in the body. Because a desire of the body is usually a stronger signal than the voice of God, the brain of a person, not learned in and not committed to the ways of God, will favor the desires of the body. It is the conflict in knowledge that destroys unity. It is the conflict in knowledge that segregates people into groups. It is the conflict in knowledge that causes people, who say they love God, to kill each other. It is the conflict in knowledge that fills prisons with people who say they believe in God. The name on the flag flown by knowledge is "conflict".

This writing is based upon information in the Bible and compatible recorded history. It is an effort to present an objective view of what Christ said about the difference in good wheat that is harvested and black kernel wheat that is destroyed. A person who trusts teachings and leaders of a religious group would be wise to remember what Christ said about the parts of the plant that are burned and the fruit of that plant that is harvested. All parts of the plant come from the same seed and all are nourished by the same life in the soil but only the part of the plant that is in the image and likeness of the parent seed is harvested. Many religious people will discover, when it is too late to correct the error, they are a part of the plant and not a duplicate of the seed that is harvested.

Christ gave John the Apocalypse (Revelation) using numbers and symbols to reveal something in time. Understanding what different numbers represent is necessary for understanding Revelation. "Original day" will designate the 24 hour days identified as such in Genesis and verified by the sun, beginning the fourth day. Secular science verifies the accuracy of the movement of objects in space. Millennial day will represent a one thousand years day.

Here are Gematria meanings to the numbers in question: 1=oneness or unity; as in one God. 2=witness-two witnesses are required to verify a statement is true. This is a common practice in modern courts of law. 3=trinity. This represents the three parts of God and man. (God-his breath-his word: Man-his breath-his word). 4=the world (earth) and its four seasons. 5=grace. Grace is something done to help someone who doesn't deserve help.

6=incomplete or unfinished. Man was created on the sixth day but was incomplete. He had not yet accepted God's proposal of love by passing the test of choice. 7=completeness.

Since nothing is ever complete in the sense of no more growth or improvement, 7 represents the completion of a phase or stage of the work planned by God. As in music, 8 is an octave of one. It repeats the first note on a higher scale. The eighth day will begin the new heaven and new earth which will be a duplicate of the first heaven and earth on a higher scale. There are an unlimited number of octaves in the repertoire of God. The first requirement in solving a problem is admitting there is a problem. It is with this attitude this author pens these words. As a member of the human race he is a part of the problem. He feels the way Isaiah the prophet felt. **Woe is me for I am undone. I am a man of unclean lips and dwell in the midst of a people of unclean lips for my eyes have seen the king, the Lord of Hosts. (Isaiah 6:5).**

ORIGINAL DAY ONE:
ONE GOD

1. Time begins (in beginning).
2. Heaven and earth are created; not ex nihil but ex-theos.
3. Everything begins as a glob of water.
4. Darkness is on the surface of this glob of water and God is beyond the darkness.
5. Light begins to exist in time.
6. God separates the light and darkness.

The word, "beginning" represents the creation of time during which a physical world and man were created. Time is the foundation of physical creation. Time does not exist in the nonphysical realm. Translating the Hebrew word shawmahyim, as heaven, causes confusion. Heaven is the abode of God but the space between the waters after God separated them is called "lofty". (1:8). Everything began as one glob of water.

Darkness covered the whole surface of this glob of water because physical light had not yet come into existence in time. God and the nonphysical world are above and beyond this darkness which covered this glob of water. His words, "Let there be light" moved the darkness away from the surface of the glob of water. At this time there was no sun and moon. Evening was the name given to darkness and morning was the name given to light after light and darkness were separated. This was before there was a sun to send light to the earth. Light became a metaphor for intelligence (the ability to see) and darkness became a metaphor for ignorance (haides-the inability to see). The space did not appear until the second day when God separated the waters with a space between them.

When God looks at creation he sees earth, and above earth, a space filled with countless objects. Some are energized by the light produced by the words, "let there be light" and others reflect light from the lighted objects. After this space, he sees the outer water which was originally one with the earth. Then he sees the darkness that once covered the glob of water. Next he sees light which emanates from him. Man has not been able to reach the outer edge of the space called "lofty" with his instruments. If he should, he would encounter the water which originally, was a part of the earth.

The distance through that water may be greater than the distance through space to this side of that water. After the water he would see a space of total darkness. Christ used this physical darkness as a parallel to to mental darkness which is ignorance. He called it "outer darkness", which acted as a holding cell for people who rejected God before his crucifixion. (Matthew 8:12; 22:13; 25:30). Peter said Christ went to them during the three days his body was in the sepulcher, to inform them they had a second chance to choose God instead of self. Christ told the apostles ignorance (hades) would not prevail against God's ability to tell a person truth the way he told Peter about Christ.

The Great White Throne Judgment was called into session after the death of Christ, where every human, who dies without love, faces a guilty verdict. Before Christ arose, a great gulf separated this area of darkness from the pleasant abode of the redeemed. (Luke 16:26). The meaning of the Greek word "haides" (hades) is "without sight". Mentally, it represents ignorance. The rich man no longer had a physical body but he wasn't blind; he could see Lazarus and Abraham who were in the light of paradise. A person in darkness can see someone who is in light just as an ignorant person can see someone who is in the light of truth. The rich man's ignorance was obvious. He asked for relief from his pain instead of asking forgiveness for that which caused his pain.

The most binding and deadly of all addictions is ignorance. It is Satan's #1 tool. It, along with Satan, will be destroyed in the Lake of Fire. The rich man thought fire was causing his pain. He no longer had a physical body so he was experiencing what a person feels when he makes an irrevocable, bad decision. The rich man chose to enjoy his material wealth without allowing Lazarus to eat crumbs that fell from the table, usually eaten by dogs. The Greek words indicate Lazarus was at the table of the rich man, eating scraps that fell from the table, before he was put outside the rich man's gate. How often does a person, who ignores the needs of his fellow man, end up in bad circumstances, and instead of confessing his sin and repenting, he asks for relief from the bad circumstances caused by his sin? A person reaps what he sows. That's a law of nature.

Many people prefer darkness to light because they don't want their evil thoughts and conduct exposed. They hide in ignorance produced by the evil part of their knowledge. They refuse to learn truth because of the pleasure ignorance gives them. Peter said this kind of person is willingly ignorant. Christ gave the reason an ignorant person is condemned. **This is the condemnation; light (intelligence) came into the world and men loved darkness (ignorance) more than the light because their conduct was evil. (John 3:19).**

This can be proven by asking people to explain their understanding of God. The most accurate information about God is found in the Bible. A person's unwillingness to learn about God from the information in the Bible makes him willingly ignorant. He will spend much time and money to qualify for a job to earn money and status but won't take a fraction of that amount of time to learn about God. Because he refuses to learn truth, he has no defense for the consequences of his ignorance.

Lofty was the name God gave the space between the glob of water he called earth and the water that was separated from the water he called the earth. This word described the great expanse between the two bodies of water. When a person looks up from the earth he sees a space filled with invisible air and beyond that he sees that space filled with innumerable objects. How big is that space?

Scientists say the ultimate speed in the universe is the speed of light which they say is about 186,000 miles per second. They say certain objects in space are millions of light years from earth. A light year is the distance light can travel in one year. Assuming light travels 186,000 miles in one second of time: 186,000 x 60 = 11,160,000 miles (one minute); 11,160,000 x 60=

669,600,000 miles (one hour); 669,600,000 x 24 =16,070,400,000 miles (one day);

16,070,400,000 x 365 = 5,865,696,000,000 miles (one year). The most important thing is not the distance but the time. If the speed of light is the ultimate speed, and scientists speak of an object a million light years away from earth, what did they use to send a signal to something that took one million years to get there and another million years to return the signal to earth? Who lived long enough to see the results?

This is another instance where the imagination of a brain produces theories not supported by common sense or fact. Scientists present much knowledge that produces good results but, when there is a contradiction between their ideas and what God says, a person is forced to choose which he will believe. Many people think what scientists say must be true because their information is beyond their understanding. Being unable to prove something is not true doesn't prove it is true. Truth is not vetted by ignorance.

Many people, who say they believe the information in the Bible, are exposed as liars by the information in the Bible. A person who doesn't believe what God told Moses about creation has no basis for saying he believes in God. It is not trusting conflicting and incomplete information but, trusting God that gives understanding. **By trusting, we mentally comprehend the word of God arraigned life; causing the result to be; what appears did not come to be from what we are seeing. (Hebrews 11:3).** Opinions not supported by fact become a substitute for truth for many who do not know or trust the information in the Bible. Yet, they say they believe in God.

Millennial Day One:
0-1000-(4,000 B. C.-3,000 B. C.)-ONE GOD

This day began with the beginning of time. Light was created in time by the words of God, "Let there be light." The word "be" eliminates the need for light to travel to be where God wanted it to be. The mistaken idea the speed of light can be used to determine the age of the universe by determining how long it takes light to travel to that object is proven false by this word "be". God put light in time on the first day. Time encompasses all of creation. Planets and other objects in space did not exist until the fourth day. God saying "Let there be light" is not like turning a light on in a room where the light has to travel.

A better word than divided is separate. Evening means mixture. Day is dawn or the un-mixing of light and darkness. A clear definition of the Hebrew word "barachias" is vague but it appears light and darkness existed together before they were separated. The sun is not a source of light but something like a lightbulb which becomes bright when energized. Darkness existing before light is the reason for the words, "evening and morning". This sequence defined the days of creation and the time which followed but, that sequence was changed by the time Christ was crucified.

Modern calendars begin and end a day when it is dark. Leviticus 23:32 is in reference to a holy day, not the sequence of night and day. Christ identified a day as consisting of twelve hours. This leaves twelve hours for the night. (John 11:9). The account of the resurrection of Christ makes dawn the beginning of a day. This sequence of day and night is seen when the two women named Mary went to look at the burial site of Christ. **Late in the Sabbath (seventh day), during the dawning of the first of the Sabbath (seven days), Mary, the Magdalene and another Mary went to**

5

look at the burial site. (Matthew 28:1). This statement states the end of the Sabbath is before the dawn of a day, not before the darkness of a night. It also clarifies the day Christ was crucified. **Just as Jonas was in the belly of the whale three days and three nights, in the same way, the son of man will be in the heart of the earth three days and three nights. (Matthew 12:40).**

Even a grade school math student can count backwards three days from Sunday morning, the first day of the new week, and arrive at Thursday. It was on Thursday when Christ said "It is finished". The remaining part of Thursday, Thursday night, Friday, Friday night, Saturday and Saturday night are three days and three nights. The fact darkness existed before light on the first original days does not mean a day begins with darkness. However, the day referred to as "The Great Day of Almighty God" began at night in Gethsemane and ended in the light of the next day. By Jewish reckoning, that was the fourth day of the week and equivalent to what happened on the "evening and morning" of the fourth original day when God put lights in the sky to guide man in his physical journey through life. Christ said he is the light of the world, who, in the form of truth, is man's mental light through life.

The morning coming before the evening is a symbol of how man began with perfect intelligence (light) and followed his desires into ignorance (darkness). Based upon the report of the women visiting the sepulcher, a day begins with a morning, not an evening or night. Evening means mixture which indicates there is some light in all darkness. This clearly represents fallen man who is a mixture of good (light) and evil (darkness). This is verified in the words of John, **"The light is shining in the darkness and the darkness is not able to take possession of it. (John 1:5).** According to the report of the two women who went to the burial site, the Sabbath may end at sundown on Saturday to accommodate a Jewish tradition but, for Christians, it ended just before dawn of the eighth day. Christ arose from the grave in the twilight of the end of the seventh day, just before dawn of the first day of the week. However, there doesn't appear to be enough importance to argue about which comes first. Some information is critical and some is not.

If certain teachings are the basis for a person's belief in God, what happens if he doesn't believe a teaching which is a part of the foundation of his faith? If a person says he believes the information in the Bible is the basis of his belief in God, what happens if he rejects the information that tells how and when God created everything? This is a question many people who say they believe in God must answer when they embrace the teachings of evolution concerning creation. The theory of evolution contradicts what God told Moses. Their error is caused by their ignorance of the ability of faith. God used the ability of faith to do what he did.

No scientific investigation can be complete or accurate until all evidence is considered. As long as scientists don't have equipment that can determine the ability of faith, their conclusions are incomplete and inaccurate.

Since God is not a physical object that can be investigated, all conclusions about him must be based upon someone's experience with him. The Bible contains information God gave Moses in a face-to-face conversation. Was this information correct? If the words of Moses were not correct why did Christ, known as the Word of God, not correct him? These words of Christ to the Jews apply to people who don't trust what God told Moses: **Don't think I will accuse you to the Father. Moses, the one in whom you place your hope, is the one who will accuse you. If you trust Moses you would trust me because he wrote concerning me. If you don't believe those writings, how can you believe my spoken words? (John 5:45-47).** Here, Christ is saying the person who doesn't believe Moses doesn't believe him.

Many in the scientific community say what Moses said isn't true and, have persuaded many who claim to be Christians, what God told Moses isn't true. Here is another example of the tree of mixed knowledge prevailing over the words of God. Many, who claim to be educated, are in this group. If these people's faith in God is based upon the information in the Bible and they don't believe the Bible, what happens to their God? If the basis for their belief in God is false, their belief in God is false. Their dedication to a religion is of no value if they do not trust information given by God.

These people are in the same position as the Jewish leaders who rejected the information given by God through Christ. If a person adjusts the information in the Bible to accommodate theories of modern scientists which contradicts the information in the Bible, he destroys his basis for believing in God.

In a parable, Christ explained the false idea held by many religious people that a person can believe God and also believe the information presented by those who contradict what God told Moses. His words identify these people. **The kingdom of heaven is compared to a man sowing good seed in his field. While the man slept, an enemy came, sowed black kernel wheat among the wheat and left. The black kernel wheat was revealed when the plants sprouted and produced fruit. Going to the master of the house the workers asked him, "Lord, didn't you sow good seed in your field? Why do you have black kernel wheat?" He answered, "An evil man did this." His workers asked, "Do you want us to gather and remove them?" He answered, "No, lest in gathering the black kernel wheat you, at the same time, uproot the wheat. Leave both to grow until the harvest and at the time of harvest I will tell the harvesters to first gather the black kernel wheat and tie it with bands to be burned and put the wheat in my storehouse." (Matthew 13:24-30).**

Harvest time is the death of the body. Many who place their confidence in people who contradict God need to face the fact, they don't believe God, they believe the people who contradict God. Will these people be able to save them from the Lake of Fire when they stand to be judged? If they have a religion that permits them to pick and choose what they want to believe; their god is the product of their knowledge. Don't be deceived by the theories of people who don't believe what God told Moses. Paul's words are appropriate here: **Don't be deceived, God is not to be mocked because, that which a man sows, that he will also reap. The person who sows into his flesh (brain/knowledge) will from his flesh reap corruption. The person who sows into the breath (the god residing in the body), from the breath he will reap the purpose of life. (Galatians 6:7-8).** Note: Aion refers to the cause or purpose of a lifespan. Aionios refers to eternal. The word here is aion. Also, eternal is not the length of life but the kind of life.

Truth is not found in incomplete and contradicting knowledge; truth is found in faith. **By trusting, we mentally comprehend the word of God arraigned life; causing the result to be; what appears did not come from what we are seeing. (Hebrews 11:3).** Knowing the information in the Bible can produce confidence based upon knowledge about the existence of God but, faith is the only way to know the reality of God. If unbelieving scientists, and people who trust them, ever learn to trust God instead of their incomplete knowledge, they will be able to see clearly how and when God did what he did. They may also see why God created man and his universe.

Whether from ignorance or persuasion by messengers of Satan, many professing Christians don't have confidence in the information in the Bible about creation. These are either black kernel wheat or a part of the plant that is not harvested. All parts of a corn plant come from the same kernel and the same soil and all the parts have a form of life but, only the kernels, which are clones of the kernel that produced the plant, are saved and put in the granary. All other parts of the plant, including the unusable black grain, are burned.

Christ repeatedly spoke of the grain, a replica of the seed from which the plant grew, being gathered for continued use and the remainder of the plant being burned. The place of this burning is the Lake of Fire which he called "The Second Death". The first death happens when, like Adam, a person deliberately rebels against the instructions of God. This causes a separation of the god in a human body from God. The second death occurs when that god who, in the time he lived in a human body, never accepted and returned God's love. He is thrown into the Lake of Fire the way a farmer throws unusable stalks into a fire to be consumed. The first death is a repairable separation from God. The second death is permanent because the person is annihilated. People who trust theories of science, religious teachings and personal beliefs need to ask if these will stand the test of truth after the death of their body.

Brilliant people, like those working on the collider to learn how the Big Bang occurred, are as suave with their speech as the cunning serpent that talked with Eve. There are many people, who are well educated, who know little if anything about God. They think their knowledge of things that apply to this world qualifies them to know about God. They think their education qualifies them to challenge what God told Moses.

Having a right to an opinion doesn't make their opinion represent truth. Life experiences have proven that many times. Just as love would not allow a spouse to have another lover, God will not allow a person, who trusts untruthful knowledge, instead of him, to be one of his. God created man and his universe to find an object upon which to bestow his love, who would love him above all else. Only people who love God are accepted by him. Love is not produced by knowledge. This allows the most uneducated person to love and be loved by God.

A strong characteristic of love is jealousy. God admitted he is jealous. Jealousy occurs when the potential for separation from a loved one is present. Not understanding this caused Adam and Eve to lose their lives and the benefits of the garden in Eden. The same kind of foolish thinking will disqualify a person for Heaven. Love allows a primary allegiance to God and a secondary allegiance to others. This can be as difficult as a woman's love for her husband causing her to choose her husband to the detriment of her children.

Since the time when religious differences caused Cain to kill Abel, many millions have died, been permanently maimed and/or had their lives wrecked because of religious differences. The brain often responds with emotion which ignores facts. It will use anger to do harm or use pride to promote self. Picture three siblings, trying to prove to each other, which of them, their parents love the most. Instead of doing things to please the parents they spend their time trying to prove which is loved the most by their parents. That's what religious people do to each other.

There are other religious beliefs in the world but the three that have similar teachings about God are Jews, Muslims and Christians. Because each is convinced God approves them over the others, they search for any available information to prove their point and apparently forget it is not their knowledge but their love for their fellow man that determines acceptance by God. **If someone says, "I love God" and hates his brother, he is a liar. If he does not love his brother who he has seen, he is not able to love God who he has not seen. (1 John 4:19).**

THE GARDEN IN EDEN

The garden in Eden did not exist during the first seven days but because it is the place where man separated from God, it will be discussed here. Much time and effort has been spent trying to locate the garden which God planted in Eden. It would be simple if the place where the four rivers forked from the one river that flowed through the garden was known. The flood changed the terrain leaving two of the rivers independent of each other. Before there was a Mediterranean Sea, a Red Sea or other water areas in the one land mass, the land identified as Eden is consistent with the land defined by a North-South longitude matching a longitude in the country of Turkey, which would align closely with Ethiopia in Africa where the Gihon flowed. The Eastern boundary would be near a longitude in the middle of modern Iran. The approximate middle of this land is in the vicinity of the Euphrates River where the Garden in Eden was located.

Because Babylon (formerly Babel) is located on the Euphrates river and because Babylon and the Euphrates river are included in things Christ revealed to John that were associated with evil, Babel is as good a choice as any as the location of the Garden. Noah and his sons knew the location of the garden. One river flowed through the land of Eden and the Garden and split into four rivers after it exited the Garden. These were Pison, Gihon (Nile), Hiddekel (Tigress) and Euphrates.

The root meaning of Babel is gate of God or gate of gods but it came to mean confusion, as in a person who babbles or speaks with meaningless words. This occurred when the people suddenly spoke different languages. Here God enabled different people to speak different languages in a moment of time. On the Day of Pentecost he allowed people with many different languages to understand one language in a moment of time. Man's ability is not limited to what his brain can do or understand.

God told Abraham he would give him the land between the Nile in Egypt and the Great River Euphrates. The Nile (Egypt) was where Israel was in bondage and the Euphrates was where the first man lived in a paradise. The Euphrates River is located in line with the one river that flowed through Eden and the garden. The Hiddekel (Tigris) is East of the Euphrates and the Pison and Gihon (Nile) are West of the Euphrates.

The Euphrates appears to be an extension of the one river that flowed through the land of Eden and the garden. Eden is a physical replica of nonphysical heaven and the river that flowed through the middle of Eden is a physical replica of the river that flows through the throne of God. The river that flows in Heaven is in the middle of a broad space. This would indicate the river in Eden flowed through the middle of the land of Eden **There was shown to me a river; water of life, clear as crystal, flowing out of the throne of God and the Lamb. In the middle of this broad space and the source of the river was a tree of life producing twelve kinds of fruit each month. Each person had his choice of fruit. The leaves were the health of the people. (Revelation 22:1-2).**

The word for great also represents great in the sense of age or reputation. A great man is not necessarily a physically big man. Since the Euphrates has existed since the days of Eden, great would appropriately represent age and reputation. Thus the four messengers bound in the Euphrates River and released would indicate Satan used all available forces, from the beginning of time to stop Christ from becoming the redemption for mankind. (Revelation 9:14). The Greek word "megas" can mean great regarding appearance. Physically it refers to size and number. Metaphorically it refers to reputation or age.

Eden was a large area. According to the locations of the four rivers, it encompassed most if not all of the Middle East and a part of Africa. Eden was eastward of some area not mentioned. Using the longitude of Ethiopia where the Gihon flowed as a landmark, east-ward would be an area east of the current Mediterranean whose longitude is similar to that of Ethiopia. Using the Euphrates as the middle of the land of Eden would make the Eastern boundary of Eden somewhere in Iran. The river mentioned in Revelation fits the description of the river in Eden. That River is in the middle of the throne and God. This indicates the river in Eden flowed through the middle of the land of Eden and, the garden was located in the middle of the land of Eden which was the throne of man before he sinned. The garden was on both sides of the river.

The flood changed the riverbeds. It eliminated the Pison or pushed it underground. It changed the course of the Gihon and extended the bed of the Hiddekel (Tigrs) northward. The statement the Gihon flowed through the whole of Ethiopia would not be possible if the Red sea was in its path. Because there was only one land mass, the Red Sea did not exist until after the flood. The land mass wasn't divided into parts until the lifetime of Peleg, sometime during the years 2243 B. C. -2004 B. C. The flood, which occurred before the division of the land mass, changed the locations of the beginnings of three of the four rivers as a landmark for the Garden in Eden. Only the Euphrates remained connected to the primary river.

Adam and Eve were exiled from the garden in Eden but not from the land of Eden. When God told Adam the land was cursed, he was speaking of all of Eden not just the Garden in Eden. A curse is a prophecy of something that will happen. It is not the words of a curse but the people to whom the curse is spoken who are responsible for causing the curse to come true. The many barren areas in the Middle East verify this curse. Land that once grew living things in abundance without any effort from man became a barren wilderness of sand. The land of Eden was what is known as the Middle East. As Adam and his descendants increasingly left God out of their daily lives, they lost their desire and ability to care for the land and, in time, much of it became waste and barren. It was easier to kill some living thing for food than plant a crop and wait for harvest.

Adam was separated from God but he still had the perfect brain God put in his head. He lost some, but not all of its ability.

The mystery of how Stonehenge and other seemingly impossible feats were accomplished would not be a mystery if people would recognize, for many centuries, people had near-perfect brains. Because their brains were only partially handicapped by the use of knowledge of evil, they were geniuses by modern standards. Levitation would have been a simple feat for them.

During this 1,000 year day, the light (truth) of God was present in Adam who lived 960 years of this first millennial day. Light is a metaphor for intelligence and truth and darkness is a metaphor for ignorance and lies. Like dawn and twilight, this knowledge became mixed with some of both. This represents what happened after Adam and Eve ate the fruit of the tree of knowledge of good and evil. Their knowledge of good and evil became mingled with their knowledge of God, causing them to be easy prey for a brilliant god, like Satan, to deceive (the meaning of Devil) them. Perfect intelligence is produced by perfect trust in God. The moment the brain is distracted from what God says is the moment a person loses the intelligence and will to resist thoughts inspired by Satan.

Satan began with Eve. He knew she would be fascinated when seeing beautiful things. He knew she liked different and special kinds of food. There was no other food like this in all of creation. These qualities are seen in the nature of a female. A man is satisfied with anything that tastes good and satisfies his hunger. A woman wants ambiance. Just as Satan wanted to be like God, he knew Eve would like to be like God and feel independent and free to make her own decisions.

Eve was partially like God. She lacked the male part of God which was necessary for her to make decisions using faith. Being programmed with a tendency to be emotional, she failed to realize being free to make choices made her responsible for her choices. Satan's desire to be like God is evidence, he was a one part being. Three things are the basic areas of temptation for a human. John described these three things as, desire of the flesh, desire of the eyes and desire for things in life that will produce admiration from others.

One thing the knowledge of good and evil did was cause them to hide their naked bodies. For some reason, appearing before others without clothes causes embarrassment for most people. The fact Adam and Eve could hear the sound of God, who is not physical, walking in the Garden, indicates he, like the wind that is a physical representation of him, was stirring the trees and vegetation. They ran for shelter. Christ explains why: **Everyone who practices evil hates the light and will not come to the light so they won't be convicted. The person doing truth continues coming to the light so his works can be verified they are being performed with God. (John 3:20-21).**

Something about learning the difference in good and evil made them want to cover their naked bodies. Because nakedness was somehow connected to an inner awareness of evil, they tried to hide their evil by hiding that which, to them, revealed they had disobeyed God. Animals do not hide their nakedness or their acts of mating. Small children are not embarrassed by nakedness until they are taught it is evil. They don't know there is a difference. Spoken or written laws are used to control inner desires that are harmful to self and/or others.

Doing something harmful is not considered evil unless some authority has forbidden it or warned against it. As Paul said, "If there is no law there is no transgression." God told them they were not to eat of the tree of knowledge of good and evil. When they refused to respect this warning from God, their punishment didn't come from God, it came from what they did. The fruit poisoned their bodies and removed their natural immunity to death. They had become like God and the beings in the nonphysical realm by knowing good and evil but, they had demonstrated, they were not qualified to control the evil part of knowledge.

To prevent them eating the fruit of the tree of life and living forever; as beings unable to cope with the knowledge of good and evil; they had to be removed from the garden. Refusal to heed God's words would now be the reason for them and their descendants being separated from life. Man would now be like a zombie controlled by a brain with limited intelligence. Imagine how much evil there would be in the world if no one died. Like Adam and Eve, children are born with immunity to nonphysical death and remain in that state until they, knowingly, and intentionally, refuse to heed the inner voice warning them what will happen if they ignore this voice. When they fail to heed the warning, they lose their immunity to death, die their first death and, become disqualified for heaven. Just as dead human bodies don't reside with living people, dead gods don't reside with living gods. After that, their only hope is grace, produced by God's love, which offers another chance to choose life.

Nakedness has been associated with evil since Adam and Eve. When the people persuaded Aaron to make a calf to worship, a part of their worship was nakedness. One aspect of evil in people is revealed by their willingness to expose their bodies. Near nude female bodies are used in the promotion of products. The nude female body is presented as something a male cannot resist. Adam was the most intelligent, wealthy and powerful man that ever lived yet, he was persuaded to trade all of that to please a nude woman. Intent is revealed by observing what a person does after the act is committed. The aprons of fig leaves were proof they knew what they did was with intent. Intent reveals guilt. Now a lie must be used to try to prove the lack of responsibility by blaming something or somebody.

Eve blamed the serpent. According to Revelation the serpent was Satan in the body of a serpent. The serpent was more cunning than any other of the creatures. Satan uses the best to do his work. After he conquered Eve he was able to enter her to conquer Adam. **The great snake, the first snake called deceiver and adversary, the one deceiving the whole earth, was thrown to the earth and his messengers with him, (Revelation 12:9). (deceiver=Devil; adversary = Satan).**

God put women in charge of the universe. They would rule by teaching boys and girls to do their bidding. When these boys and girls became men and women, they would live by the teachings of their mothers. Women, designed by God to deal with babies and children, are naturally naïve and slow to suspect someone might not be telling them the truth. Even when she knows someone is lying, she looks for an excuse for their conduct. Eve listened to the serpent with a trusting ear. Now she is blaming the serpent for what she did. The serpent got his comeuppance. He and man became deadly enemies and he and his descendants would have to spend their lifetime crawling on their bellies.

This tendency to believe without question is the reason females should remain with the assignment God gave them with children. The lies of children seldom do great harm. Adam blamed Eve who was, originally, a part of him. A strong test of love is a willingness to not blame the person loved even though they may have influenced what happened. Influence is never equal to an act. At this time the female part of Adam had been removed and given a different body. Now, Adam was 100% male but not 100% man; his female part was missing. Also, a real man does not blame a woman for something he does. When it comes to accepting responsibility, a man is a male but a male may not be a man.

The penalty for the serpent has been decreed, now it is time for the woman to receive her sentence. Because she recklessly made a decision beyond her authority, God told her she needed a supervisor. She would be subject to Adam, be more anxious when faced with decisions and, her pregnancies would increase. Anxiety strongly interferes with objective thinking. The psychic and emotional system God put in women makes them the best teachers and comforters of children and husbands but, this unique ability becomes a handicap if they have to make difficult decisions affecting adult situations.

Pregnancies represent the power of sexual desire by both, men and women. Adam and Eve had many more children than those mentioned. Because a woman desires the pleasure a man can give her, she isn't able to control how often she becomes pregnant. Today billions of dollars are spent on drugs and apparatuses to prevent pregnancies and when this doesn't work, the fetus is sometimes destroyed. Eve had always been an equal partner with Adam. Now, not only will she be drawn to him, he will be her boss. Equal authority with men pursued by women is a violation of this decree of God. However, many women enjoy equality given them by a husband who loves them. Love is the only thing that makes people equal and man equal with God. When a man loves a woman, his love not only makes her equal, it makes him her voluntary slave.

The murder of Abel by Cain is evidence Eve didn't do the job God assigned her. The quality of performance of women to do the job God assigned them is seen in the speech and conduct of their children. Daycares, schools and churches cannot do what mothers can do. Most of the teachings of religious organizations are the history of their movement and promotions of their agendas. Repetitious teachings of history are like reruns on TV; in time they become boring and uninspiring. It is the "never knowing what they will do next" of a child that gives a mother endless opportunities to partner with God in the teaching and training of a child. This world offers nothing as satisfying and prestigious as being a partner with God.

It is not hearing a sermon about God but seeing a sermon in a mother that goes with the child into adulthood and old age. A proverb says the same thing; **"Discipline a child in the way he should go and he will not change when he is old." (Proverbs 22:6).** The two things required for successful discipline are pain and pleasure administered with love. If dumb animals can be trained using this method, surely any normal child can be trained. A parent's refusal to apply appropriate pain for bad conduct is evidence their love for their child is not as great as their love for self. A parent, refusing to apply appropriate penalty by hiding behind emotion, can leave a child unprotected from demonic forces manipulating his thoughts. The conduct of children, approved by parents, may not be approved by God.

Adam blaming Eve didn't impress God. Since he decided to eat of the tree of knowledge of good and evil, his life would now be guided by knowledge in his brain instead of God. Some knowledge would show him how to produce good and some would show him how to produce evil. He would have to rely upon a brain biased toward itself and its body for a decision. Being separated from God (the meaning of death), his brain, not him, would be the one to make the choices. The more knowledge his brain collected, the more he would trust his brain. His brain was filled with conflicting information that produced indecisiveness and made it difficult to choose knowledge that would produce good results. Christ told the apostles he would return as truth which would enable a person to again, receive advice from God. He began doing that almost 2,000 years ago.

Instead of the luxurious, natural growth of Eden, Adam will now have to till the ground filled with thorns and briars. Instead of the delicacies of a king which he ate in Eden, which grew without any effort from him, he will now see thorns and briars growing where delicious food once grew. He will now have to toil to persuade the ground to give him food. While he is waiting for his crop to mature he will eat the grass that grows naturally or kill something for food. From eating like a king, he went to eating like a cow or a beast. Faith, not knowledge gives man the ability to navigate the earth and the adjacent systems surrounding it. Now that which God placed under his authority will act on its own.

Earth is like a huge space ship with controls that won't respond to man's carnal knowledge. It was designed to respond to faith-thoughts and Adam no longer had faith. Instead of conversations with God in the cool of the evening, he now has to rely upon a brain made of dirt to tell him what to do. Instead of the comfortable temperature of Eden, he will eat his meals with sweat running down his face. Knowledge of evil doesn't prevent evil or solve problems caused by evil. No person can be helped until he is willing to do what is necessary to help himself. He may know the difference in good and evil but his brain, biased toward its knowledge and the desires of its body, can only be subdued by truth which is good knowledge

Knowing good and evil is less of a problem for a person who knows and has confidence in what God says. Truth is good and a lie is evil. Knowing good and evil puts man on the same level as God (3:22). It is not good and evil but how a person responds to good and evil that makes him like God or like Satan. Drugs, alcohol, fame, fortune, beautiful women and handsome men are everywhere. The response to these and other things like them determines respect for self, others and God.

God equipped Eve to help her children experience love. He placed her under the supervision of Adam so she and her children could experience voluntary submission which is necessary for someone handicapped by conflicting information. Obviously, she would not be able to set an example of love and submission if she didn't love and respect the words of God. Her desire to satisfy her physical body, her desire to look at beautiful things and her desire to be intelligent, overcame her respect for the instructions of God. The irony of Eve's foolish decision was; she already had everything Satan was promising her. The most treasured trophy sought by humans and God, is contentment. This is not found in an ability to create or own things; it is only found when a man, a woman and God experience mutual love.

The first wages she earned for her sin was losing her relationship with God, her source of life. The second was learning her husband didn't love her. He blamed her for what he did. The third was losing her home and queenly way of life. The fourth was when one of her sons killed his brother. "Don't do as I do; do what I say" has never been successful as a teaching method. Truth can be a light for the best path for life but it cannot make a person walk that path. Light can reveal evil but it cannot prevent a person embracing evil. Knowledge used by a human brain contains both truth and lies and is the ideal setting for a naïve person to become food for Satan who Peter described as a lion looking for a meal. (1 Peter 5:8).

If knowledge is the primary goal for a child, many people can do that, some better than a mother. With all the things knowledge provides, many use it as the foundation for life and that is why there is so much conflict in the world. Different knowledge makes people think and act differently. The universal language which enables people with different knowledge to agree is love. God's foundation for life is love. Love cannot be taught; it can only be experienced. Knowledge is subject to change but an experience remains the same. A child does not forget love experienced with a mother.

Love is not subject to race, culture or religion. Every mother is qualified to lay the foundation of love. It is not the teachings of Judaism, Islam, Christianity etc. that touches God's heart, it is love. The religions of this world may teach information beneficial for activity in this world but they can't lay the foundation of love which is essential for the revival of life lost by sin. Because so many mothers left their post, Satan has been able to use religion as his most destructive force. All religions teach love but being taught about love is not the same as experiencing love which begins when a new god is being formed in the womb of a mother.

A mother and father have two separate assignments. If either fails, the child pays the price for their failure. A child needs to learn tolerance and compassion from a mother and pragmatic thinking and firmness from a father. If a father is missing or does not have these qualities, the male child will not learn the characteristics of a man. He will not have the non-emotional, pragmatic, self-confident attitude required for tough decisions.

A female child will not have the experience of feeling safe because of the strength and toughness of a father who values her life above his. When this happens, both male and female child will not experience what God wants them to experience. They may be exceptional because of their knowledge but, without love, they will fail to reach the potential God planned for them. One of the greatest insults against God is when two males or two females think they can do the assignment God gave to a mother and father.

Because they think their intelligence qualifies them to challenge the authority of God, many women seek the assignments God gave men. It is not intelligence but authority that determines who is boss. Just as Lucifer wanted to be like God, many women want to be like a man by occupying the place God assigned to man. The women who do this, trade the most important of all God's assignments for something that will perish with time. Their children are taught information by someone other than a mother. Being deceived into thinking knowledge meets all needs; instructions replace the unique relationship of a mother and child. These women are admired, not as mothers faithful to God's instructions, but as successes in a secular world. This is a pitifully, foolish way to waste a life.

Not only Seth but other sons and daughters were born to Adam and Eve. Does that mean brothers and sisters bore children? Yes. Incest was a common practice for at least the first 2,000 years. Sarah was Abraham's half-sister. Moses commanded marriages be within the same tribe. Marrying cousins and other relatives was common 2500 years after Adam and Eve. Just because customs evolve doesn't mean older customs were wrong. Laws and traditions are made by men who often, only know the word "god" not the person who is God.

Cain killing Abel was just the first thing mentioned of Eve's failure to do what God designed her to do. There were two moral codes that produced life and death. God represented the one that produced life and Satan represented the one that produced death. It would seem after one son murdered another, she would have learned the tragic error of trusting her knowledge instead of what God told her. She no doubt told her children of her foolish decision but they, following her example, yielded to similar curiosities of knowledge. The first 1,000 years saw her, her female children and their descendants fail many times.

When desires of the body and emotions of the brain join forces, the result is almost always, a rejection of God's advice. The desires of perfect bodies and the emotional reasoning of perfect brains caused Adam and Eve to reject the warnings of God. That should be a warning to people with imperfect bodies and imperfect brains, of the force they face when a demon comes calling. Because they were separated from God (dead) after they sinned, God had to communicate with them by causing thoughts to appear in their brains. Christ told the apostles he was truth and would return to them as the Breath of Truth. A thought appearing in the brain representing truth is Christ speaking. He gives knowledge that will produce good results. The brain judges that thought by its existing knowledge and chooses between that thought and its existing knowledge. Only a person, who trusts God more than existing knowledge, will act upon the instructions of Christ.

The human brain, with an egocentric mixture of truth and lies, is protective of its information. When God communicates with a thought, the brain must decide to accept or reject that thought. It will oppose any challenge to its categories of information that is used as a basis for opinions. This is why it is important to know the information in the Bible which contains information about God. A slight adjustment to George Santayana's words is apropos. "He who is ignorant of history is doomed to repeat it."

The emotional reasoning of a human brain produced the first killing caused by religious differences. The religious responses of Cain and Abel, to God, were different. Instead of taking his problem to God, Cain decided to challenge Abel about his way of making an offering. Abel couldn't solve Cain's problem with God any more than one religious person can solve another religious person's problem with God. Abel, agreeing with Cain, would not have solved Cain's problem with God. If a person has a problem, the solution is found by working it out with God, not by attacking someone who thinks differently. God told Cain, if he didn't do that, he would end up ruling over sin. Every person is a ruler over good and evil. Some, like Adam and Eve try to blame something or someone when they make a bad decision but they alone were in charge of the choice that produced the outcome. They were the rulers over a choice that produced evil.

The idea evil controls a person is not supported by this statement of God. Each person's brain controls his thoughts and conduct. Repentance is not a change of conduct but a change of attitude which controls the brain, that controls thought, that controls conduct. If a person embraces the ways of God, the wellbeing of others will be important to him. If he rejects the ways of God, doing and getting what he wants will be his goal. Both, good and evil will always be standing in front of him waiting for him to make a choice. Because the brain of each person controls his/her choices, a religious person's brain may manipulate information to arrive at a choice based upon existing or biased reasoning instead of what God says.

ORIGINAL DAY TWO: WITNESS

1. God separated the single glob of water.
2. He put a space between the two bodies of water and called the space "lofty".

At first, there was one glob of water. God divided the one glob into two parts and put a space between the two. Because this space surrounds the water that became earth, it is reasonable to assume the outer portion of water encircles the space that encircles earth. The part that moved away became a covering of water, beyond the space. The space between the two bodies of water was called "lofty" or "high". Translations that call this space heaven cause confusion. Heaven is the timeless abode of God. The distance between the earth and the outer edge of this space has never been determined. On the fourth original day it was filled with innumerable objects, many larger than earth

Here is an idea about the size of this space. The earth is a tiny ball with a circumference of almost 25,000 miles. Its rotation causes its surface to move about 1,375 miles per hour. The earth's atmosphere rotates with the earth to keep things from blowing off the surface. The earth, with its atmosphere, is moving about 75,000 miles per hour in its orbit around the sun. The sun, as it relates to other space objects, is moving about 45,000 miles per hour. The speed of earth traveling through space is about 1,860,000 miles per hour. (Casey Research).

There are approximately 52,560,000 hours in 6,000 years. Not counting the miles earth has traveled around the sun, the highway miles earth has traveled through space is about eight trillion, 409 billion, 600 million miles (8,409,600,000,000). Earth is a tiny piece of its galaxy. Wherever it is going, it hasn't passed any other planets or neighboring galaxies and there is no evidence earth is anywhere near the outer limit of space. That would be the first leg of the journey; the next would be the great distance through the water and then through the darkness. Different information may give different results but whatever the conclusion, a person becomes dumbstruck when he tries to imagine the ability of God to construct something this big. Traveling at the speed of light would make visiting the next door neighbor an impossible trip for the life span of a human but, traveling at the speed of thought would take less time than it takes to say, "Let's go visit our neighbor."

At this time the earth was nothing but water. The teaching that life on the earth came from water is verified by this information but, the answer is not complete until God is credited with being the source and controller of the water. The water was the means; God was the cause. Air, which is physical and a metaphor for God's breath, surrounds the earth like a shield to keep objects in space from harming the earth. The great speed of an object approaching earth causes enough friction, while passing through the air, to burn most if not all of the object.

This is one of many messages God put in the heavens to tell humans he is protecting them from enemies much larger and more powerful than they. God can protect a person from anything except himself. The water which was a part of the first phase of creation and separated from the water called "earth", is now beyond this space with all the objects.

MILLENNIAL DAY TWO:
1,000-2,000 (3,000 B. C.-2,000 B. C.) WITNESS

Two represents a viable witness. In a court of law, two witnesses are required to validate a testimony. On original day two God separated the core of the mass of water he created, from the rest of the water and put a permanent space between the two so vast, man, with all his instruments, cannot see the outer edge of this space. How well does the knowledge of an organism, seen only with a powerful microscope, compare with the knowledge of a well-educated human adult? If compared with God, man is like that tiny microscopic organism. There is no way he can understand God with knowledge but, like a small child is to a parent, trusting the parent doesn't require understanding. The earth and the seemingly, unlimited space above earth are two witnesses to the unlimited ability of God. That happened on original day two.

Millennial day two has two witnesses to the unlimited power of God concerning earth. Man was given the universe and the authority of faith to control it. Man's conduct destroyed his faith and his authority over the universe; a part of which was the forces of nature on earth. Christ demonstrated the control Adam had over nature before Adam separated from God. After Adam lost his faith, God held nature in check so it wouldn't destroy mankind. The flood demonstrated what happens when God removes his hand from nature. The second witness of God's power was when he divided the one land mass into continents. The flood and the separation of the land are two witnesses in millennial day two of the unlimited authority of God over earth. The power that enforces this authority is faith.

God is mentally understood as being something like air or breath. As breath he created Adam in his image and likeness. As breath he spoke to Moses and the prophets and was put into the physical body of Christ where his breath was translated by Christ's vocal chords into words so man, retarded to the level of his brain, could clearly hear and understand the voice of God. That is why John called Christ "The Word of God" and why Christ said, **"All authority in heaven and earth was given to me."** Christ's words were backed up by the authority of God which was demonstrated by his ability to release nature to clean the earth of evil people and, the separation of the one land mass.

Seth, the third son of Adam, was born when Adam and Eve were 130 years old. He lived 912 years and died in 2958 B. C., 82 years after the death of his father Adam. The information Adam had about creation, the Garden in Eden, the eviction from the garden and events of almost all of the first 1,000 years, was firsthand knowledge for Seth. Noah was born in 2944 B. C. near the beginning of the second millennial day and lived 600 years during the lifetime of Methuselah who lived 273 years during the lifetime of Adam. Noah lived 950 years which was almost all of the second millennial day. Two men; Adam and Noah; had first-hand knowledge of the first 2,000 years.

This should eliminate any questions about the accuracy of biblical information that tells what God did. Even though the people turned away from God, they would still know the information about things God did. Based upon the ages of certain people listed in Genesis, the flood happened in 2344 B. C. Methuselah died in the year of the flood and his name represents what happened. Meth means full grown and thuselah is a weapon of destruction. The flood was a full grown weapon of destruction.

There is no need to become impatient with people who are confident the world has been here millions of years because all conclusions have to be based upon confidence in acquired information. The scientists have confidence in their theories which originated in some person's imagination and verified by instruments designed to agree with their imagination. A person who is confident the information God gave Moses in a face-to-face meeting is true, can look at the earth, sky and self and see undeniable evidence of the truth of what he reads in Genesis.

Confidence is the product of compatible information. Confidence is not proof. There is an intelligence that does not require information and can only be acquired by experience. That is the intelligence of love. It has innumerable witnesses it exists but, the only detectable evidence, is what is does. It can't be detected with any equipment made by man. It cannot be produced, controlled or destroyed by man yet, there is no doubt it exists. Love is often confused with the mental emotion called "like" which is produced by information and circumstances.

Love has many children but the first and most powerful child is faith. Just as there is no equipment that will prove the existence of love, there is no equipment that will prove the existence of faith. Compatible information can produce confidence concerning God but faith is required to produce understanding of and an acquaintance with God. That's why it is useless to debate something caused by faith with a person who does not recognize faith as the force used in creating man and his universe.

Faith is what God used to create the universe. Faith is what humans use to gain access to and, an understanding of God. Confidence comes from compatible information but faith comes from love. People may debate the pros and cons of creation but the person who experiences love doesn't need to debate; love provides him with faith which gives him understanding. **By trusting, we mentally comprehend the word of God arraigned life; causing the result to be; what appears did not come to be from what we are seeing. (Hebrews 11:3).** God is love. He is not physical so, until scientists invent an instrument that can detect love, they cannot detect God and accurately identify faith which enabled him to perform a full grown act of creation in the time it took him to think. The ultimate speed is not the speed of light; the ultimate speed is the speed of thought.

A person is killed by a weapon. Instruments can identify the weapon that did the killing but they cannot detect the force in the person that caused him to fire the weapon unless the person tells them. A person gives his fortune to needy people. The gift and what it does can be ascertained but the force in the person who gave the gift cannot be detected by manmade instruments. The instruments of scientists cannot measure love or faith, they can only measure what love and faith produces. As long as they don't include faith as the cause of creation, they will provide bogus results concerning creation.

A true believer is a person who has received the gift of love from God. With or without the information in Genesis, he understands this universe was created by a super intelligent force. God, talking face-to-face with Moses, eliminates any question about the possibility of faulty memory of people who lived the 2500 years between the beginning and Moses. Each person must choose who they will believe. Because knowledge has so much influence over people, many who claim to be believers in God, choose to trust the knowledge of scientists or a person with a reputation, instead of what God told Moses. These people try to have it both ways so they won't appear ignorant to academia. They make themselves liars by claiming to believe the God of the Bible while embracing the theories of evolution which contradict the Bible. Their "educated" teachers are some of the false prophets used by Satan to deceive people.

Lofty was the name God gave to the space between the glob of water he called earth and the water that was separated from the water he called the earth. When a person looks up from the earth he sees a lofty space filled with invisible air and beyond that, he sees that space filled with innumerable shining objects. The source of light for these objects is God. Some are energized by the force of the original light, like a lightbulb is by electrical current, and some reflect that light. Their light reflects the glory of God the way the moon reflects the glory of the sun.

Beyond this space God called Lofty, is the water that originally, was a part of the earth. No one but God knows how much water is out there. Beyond the water is the darkness that prevailed in the beginning. When God ordered light, the light did not destroy the darkness it moved it away from the glob of water. Then, as a reminder of the existence of the original darkness when there was no life, he positioned the sun and earth as a daily reminder of the life, light could give. It also shows how ignorance (darkness) can be overcome by intelligence. (Light). Christ is the light of the world. As Paul said, some of the people who sat in darkness have seen this great light.

After the separation of the water, the earth part was nothing but water and it was scattered in the space called Lofty. Then God gathered this water into one place and dehydrated enough of it to produce a dry substance that covered about 1/3 of the total surface. This dry substance was called "dry" and came to be called "land". After the first seven original days the grass and trees were growing. The trees were not a problem but who was going to cut the grass? Man had not yet received a physical body. (Genesis 2:5).

It isn't difficult for an unbiased human brain to believe the information in the Bible but, believing the bazaar theories of people who oppose God by ignoring factual knowledge of people whose lives overlapped hundreds of years and, challenging the information God so carefully gave mankind through Moses, the Prophets and Christ, is the arrogant thinking of a fool. The human brain is a piece of dirt designed to operate a human body. If it does not have sufficient intelligence to control itself and protect its body, why does it think it can know what God did without accepting vetted witnesses? In addition to the experiences many people have had with God, both the earth and sky are full of trustworthy witnesses. **The skies explain the splendor of God and the visible arch of the sky announces his achievements. Psalm 19:1**

Sometime, between 2243 B. C. and 2004 B. C., the single land mass that originally came from the glob of water called earth was divided into what is now known as continents and islands. The author of an article in a 1969 edition of National Geographic gave the opinion of many, who believed the continents and islands were originally one land mass. The waters of the flood rose above the tops of the mountains. Some of the water came from rain but most of it came from converting the soil back to water. When the earth was nothing but water God converted water to dry land. If he can do that, he can liquefy dry land to make water.

Just prior to the flood, the imaginations of all but eight of the people on earth reached a point of being continually evil. Now, removed 100+ years from the destruction of the flood, the descendants of the survivors of the flood were again in conflict because of their mixed knowledge. Knowledge of what the flood did and why it happened had little if any influence on them. Without faith to include God in their agenda, conflicting knowledge forced them to form the first recorded democratic government. Their goal was a government of the people, by the people and for the people. Does this sound familiar? The first recorded democratic form of Government was more than 4,000 years ago in a place appropriately called "Babel". Babel means "gate of God" or "gate of gods". It came to mean "confusion" which appropriately describes a government of the people, for the people and by the people.

In this kind of Government the majority can vote for or against anything, including God. This is seen in the people who make decisions for America. There was a direct line of communication from Adam, who knew the location of the garden, and Nimrod, the great grandson of Noah who was the founder of Babel. Babel is the most reasonable place where the garden existed. These people in Babel were convinced they had sufficient knowledge to make good decisions. It should be noted these people lost much of the perfect intelligence of Adam but they were still superior in intelligence to modern man.

Man's superior intelligence began declining when Adam chose a diet of knowledge instead of faith. As God told Adam, "You prefer the tree of knowledge: that will be your food." The food for the god part of Adam was the words of God. This is confirmed by Christ who quoted Moses, **"He humbled you, by allowing you to be hungry, and fed you with manna which, neither you or your fathers understand so, he might make you understand, man does not only live by bread but by every word that proceeds out of the mouth of the Lord. (Deuteronomy 8:3; Luke 4:4).**

The word manna is the word "what". The people were asking, "What is this?" It was the word of God in the form of bread which sustained life for the god living in the human body. The brains of the people were so dysfunctional they could not transfer words of God to the inner man so God provided an alternate route through the digestion system. The statement, "You are what you eat" applies to the physical, mental and nonphysical parts of a person. Christ told the people he was the bread of life which came from heaven. He stunned the people by telling them, eating his flesh and drinking his blood was necessary for life. His body and blood were produced by the word of God and therefore, was the same as the manna. He used this symbolism at the last supper when he told the apostles the bread was his body and the wine was his blood.

In the wilderness, manna was the morning meal for the god living in the body. In the afternoon the quail were food for the physical body. If the god part of a person is deprived of his morning meal (manna from God), he will be compelled to rely upon the conflicting and incomplete information in his brain, for his decisions for the day. Perhaps this is the origin of the saying, "Breakfast is the most important meal of the day." Starving people have little, if anything, to contribute to themselves or others.

Democracy wields the will of the majority of the people who make the decisions. When the majority is people who think they believe God, no matter how wrong they are, they are convinced the outcome is approved by God. Often they are as wrong as the Scribes and Pharisees who crucified Christ and Peter who murdered a man and his wife over money.

When a person measures self by what he has instead of what he is, his goal is to acquire as much fame, fortune and power as he can. The standard for success becomes doing things that are bigger and better than achievements of others. The people in Babel, who replaced God with their imaginations and ambitions, needed to prove themselves by having the biggest and tallest buildings, the most powerful military, the most wealth, the biggest and best of everything. Their ignorance of God prevented them seeing this also means the biggest and worst of things that are evil which will erode and destroy the good they desired. America is much like Babel. She builds the biggest and best and, in spite of her obviously, evil ways, leaders who are products of her church system, keep her thinking God approves.

Agenda oriented leaders adjust God's words about love to justify the use of violence against those who disagree with them and, protect criminals who do evil. Democracy represents a divided people who cooperate out of necessity or common cause, not out of love. The differences in knowledge are reconciled by concession, not by agreement. Confusion separates the people of America. Her "towers of Babel" are meaningless because her people's cooperation is based upon a desire for prosperity instead of love. Wealth is considered proof of intelligence.

The people of Babel reached an agreement to join together and build a super-sized building that would reach higher into the lofty space than any other. Man, like God, has a desire to produce something spectacular. The difference is the purpose of the deed. God did not make this universe for himself but for the pleasure of someone he loved. If Adam had not sinned, man could travel anywhere in the universe with the speed of thought. This motive of doing something to please another is seen in parents who strive to provide good things for their children. It is seen in some men and women whose primary goal is to please their spouse. It was not the building of the high tower but the reason for building it that revealed the evil of the people of Babel. They wanted to make a name for themselves.

This same zeal for status is seen in men and women who neglect spouse and children to provide extra for the spouse and children. The driving force is not love of family but love of status. A people who care for each other put each other first. This makes everyone more than themselves and, in time, all are great without trying to be great. Greatness is not found in status, wealth and power but in a love for people. This is what makes God great. Many who live in poverty of things are great because they are wealthy in love for people and people who love them.

In the Apocalypse (Revelation), Christ identified the three forces that control all of humanity except the Chosen. People in these three groups build buildings to represent who they are. Each group has a particular type of architecture. There is a conspicuous architecture for government buildings, another for religious buildings and a third for commercial buildings. The buildings identify the agenda of the people in the buildings. The size of the building and quality of the building material, represent their wealth and influence. These buildings are images, of what the people who built them consider important. They represent the pyramid system (600-60-6) used by world organizations to conduct their businesses. They are images of the beast. (See Revelation).

Religion is the most evil of the three because it claims to represent God. In the Christian religion; instead of obeying the instructions of Christ to individually share the love of God, it markets its selections of teachings like a business marketing a product, to find customers who will help it become wealthy and influential. The size and quality of its building is one of its selling tools. Like the people of Babel, all are eager to "make a name for themselves." Christ said a tree is known by the fruit it bears. Religion is the tree from which government and commerce are produced. The character of people in government and commerce are reflections of the character of people in religion. Almost every government person is a member of some church or religion.

Democracy reflects the desires of a majority of the leaders of the people. Laws made by the majority become more sacred than the words of God. When there is a conflict, the law takes authority over God. People relied upon laws to justify robbing, enslaving and killing the Indians who owned the lands of America. Laws justified enslaving and killing Negroes. Laws make it right for leaders, selected by the people, to make laws that benefit them but not the people. Laws make it legal to take the possessions of the one who earned them and give them to another who did nothing to deserve them. There is no limit to the potential evil of people who rely upon laws. Nice words and good deeds do not negate the evil of this substitute for the authority of God.

God produced a condition that caused the people to scatter and join with people who spoke the same language. Like Eve, the people of Babel took authority without sufficient intelligence to properly use authority. As humans with imaginations produced by brains made of dirt, nothing would restrain them and, in time, they would destroy themselves. By scattering them across, what was then one land mass, the few who remembered God could make their own decisions without being coerced or bribed by laws enforced by a democracy. They could again ask God for guidance for their lives. Democracy does not make people equal; only love does that, and God is the only source of love. Democracy is born with the innocence of a new born baby who grows up to become "public enemy # 1".

God did what needed to be done to save the people from themselves. He installed different languages in them so people who thought alike could communicate and work together for the good of everyone in the group. The longer people who think differently work together, the more they compromise their principles. In time there is no individual thinking and decisions are made according to the consensus of the group. Egocentric people gradually enlist enough people to become a majority and make decisions that favor what they want.

The most subtle of the three primary world forces (religion, government and commerce) is religion. It presents itself as representing a loving and truthful God but adjusts what God says to accommodate the wishes of people. Religion has many of the characteristic of commerce and government. All seek unity but don't seem to understand, unity is not produced by laws, persuasion or money. Unity is produced by people whose love enables them to compromise without resentment. This is not difficult when a person loves another the way he loves himself.

Whether it is a dictatorship, democracy, a religious hierarchy or some other form of human controlled authority, the people must approve for it to exist. The end result is a replacement of God with flawed human knowledge. The Lord said to Samuel, **"Listen to the voice of the people and do what they tell you because, they**

have not rejected you; they have rejected me to prevent me reigning over them." (1 Samuel 8:7). Look at America and other nations of the world; these words are as true today as they were when they were first spoken.

Good is produced when people listen to God. Evil is produced when people listen to Satan and, Satan has more people speaking for him than God. The world might have an outside chance of having peace if people with the same beliefs stayed separated from people who think differently. No nation, whose people have different objects of worship, different moral standards and different languages, can become one. There is not that much love in human nature.

Millions of men and women marry, who ignore differences to accommodate a physical desire or emotional need. They either divorce or live an unhappy and unfulfilled life. A mixture of good and evil knowledge, which requires compromise that forsakes basic beliefs, can produce wasted lives. Freely choosing to follow God's advice without requiring others to do the same is the only way to overcome negative emotional responses of a brain, filled with good and evil information toward someone who thinks and acts differently.

The number two represents a viable witness. The flood and separation of the one land mass are two acceptable witnesses to the unlimited authority of God over all his creation except man. Man must be free of all authority, except his own, if he is to make an acceptable decision to accept or reject God's love. Love cannot be produced with coercion, bribery or force. Man is free to accept and enjoy God's love from the distance of faith or, be like the insects crawling over dead bodies to reach the utopia of what he thinks knowledge can do for him.

The light of knowledge will always attract humans. Whether it benefits or harms them depends upon the source of their knowledge and how they use it. The rewards of knowledge acquired for the purposes of fame, fortune and power are, disappointment, tragedy and death. The rewards of knowledge whose source is God are, pressure from a carnal brain, shunning by worldly people, a non-provable faith, love, joy, peace and an endless life with God. Satan has more knowledge than all humans combined but he no longer has access to God. Knowledge without God is a dead end street. God is the only source of knowledge that doesn't become extinct. He is the only light that won't destroy those who seek him. He is a life boat for any who are willing to trust him more than the sinking ship of carnal knowledge. The words of prophets are used by Paul to explain the need for separation by God's people.

What does the temple of God have in common with idols? We are the Holy of Holies of God. We are alive. It is as God said, "I will dwell in them and walk with them. I will be God to them and they will be my people." For this reason God is saying, "Come out from them and set a boundary. Don't cling to them and I will receive you. I will be a father to you and you will be my sons and daughters." Almighty God is saying this. (2 Corinthians 6:16-18). This is impossible to do physically in a society where livelihood comes from employment by people with different ways of thinking but, not in the areas of speech and conduct. Separation by speech and conduct is an effective way to exhibit what trusting God does for a person.

The worship of idols is more common than many think. An idol is a physical object or image which represents a human idea of a deity. Reverent admiration of this object or image is idolatry. If the reader is a Jew, how does he feel toward a scroll of the Torah, a synagogue or rabbi? If the reader professes being a Christian, how does he feel about the Bible, a cross, a minister or a church building? If the reader is a Muslim how does he feel about the Quran, a mosque or an imam? God instructed nothing should be made to represent him. Christ worked about 3 ½ years without building a building, adopting a symbol or organizing a group other than the apostles who were instructed to act as individuals. The instructions to the seventy pairs he sent out were not to organize a church or start a movement; they were messengers telling the people they met; "The reign of God has arrived".

Christ was a witness of the reality of God and he empowered certain people to do as he was doing. Because a group needs a place to meet, church buildings have to be built or rented. Because this building is the place where people meet for religious activity, the building begins to be considered a holy place and an object of special respect and admiration. Christ's description of the small wild animal (beast) and his image fits the description of the pyramid systems and their buildings. Christ had the ability to have the finest earth had to offer but, as he said, **foxes have holes and the birds of the air have their nests but, the son of man has no place to lay his head.** What would a sophisticated America think of a leader who appeared to be that poor?

An idolater is not necessarily a bad person. He may have many good traits but having good traits doesn't outweigh his affection for an object or image associated with his worship of God. Satan blinds him to the psychological fact a religious object can affect the brain, causing it to produce an emotional response which is mistaken for admiration for God. It becomes an obstacle between him and God and interferes when Christ, as the Holy Breath of God, tries to communicate with him. Crosses on steeples, in church yards and on personal items are supposed to represent Christ but they violate the instructions of God. Also, to revere some translation of the Bible to the point of believing it is perfect is idolatry. To think a "holy book" or symbol has some magical influence is idolatry. To admire Mary, the pope, Muhammad or some other leader as being someone more loved by God, is idolatry.

God loves all people the same but In the 2,000 years since Christ brought the pure (good) knowledge of God into the world, church people have so mingled good and evil knowledge, few understand what worship of God is. Instead of following the instructions of Christ to be individual witnesses, people form groups and the consensus of the group determines what is to be done. Instead of individuals doing what God instructs them to do; they are like the people of Israel who wanted a king to tell them what to do. Groups become religious systems who spend their time marketing their teachings to enlist people to their way of thinking. Love is not a teaching and expressions of love are not discriminatory.

Christ said the Father (God) seeks people who will worship him in breath and truth. Breath (incorrectly translated spirit) is the person living in the body who is a nonphysical breath-being like God. He receives communication from God, Satan and other human breaths. Religious services use knowledge to appeal to the brains of the participants. Emotion produced by the brain is often thought to be the Holy Breath (spirit) of God. The god living in the body is the only part of a human that can worship God. Worship is not activity; worship is a sharing of love. Worship of God is like two people who love each other spending time together. It is not what is said or done but the togetherness that constitutes worship. This is worship in breath and truth. Nothing else is needed.

The time is coming and has already arrived when the true worshippers will worship the Father in breath and truth. The Father is looking for those worshipping this way. God is breath and it is necessary for those who worship him, worship in breath and truth. (John 4:23-24). Just as traditions in Judaism blinded the Jews and traditions in Islam blinded the Muslims; traditions in the church system have blinded people who think religious rituals are worshipping God. None appear to realize, this activity, while generating emotion in the brain, increases the difficulty of recognizing the voice or presence of God. Unfortunately, a blind person can't see what he doesn't see.

Religions, including the church system, rely upon knowledge to devise teachings, activities and programs to satisfy the need of the human brain to look to someone greater than self. God is not an idea; he is a living being. Worship is a sharing of love. Worshipping God is, loving God. No activity is required. Love is not an emotion produced by the brain; it is something experienced by the breath-being that lives in a human body. Like is not love. Like is controlled by conduct and circumstances; love is not controlled. Love for a person or love for God is a gift given to certain people by God. He is the only one who knows the person who will return his love.

If Peter had done what Christ told him, he would not have started something that would deceive so many people. He would have shared his experiences with God and, like a rock dropped into water, he would have made a wave and that wave would have made another and so on until the message of God would spread across the earth. Instead, he became the pebble Christ called him, moved along by the stream of ambition and circumstances. The human brain is not designed to love so; a person cannot worship God with anything produced by the brain.

Like the Jews and Muslims, people in the church system think anyone who does not embrace their belief is an infidel. People in the church system center their faith upon the name "Jesus" without being told by leaders who know; Jesus is not the correct human name for Christ. Here again is an instance when tradition is preferred to truth. Peter said there was none other name under heaven by which we can be saved. The name recorded in the Greek text is Iesous, not Jesus. He was not saying belief about a name would save someone, he was saying the person represented by the name will save someone. Believing the president's name is Trump doesn't do anything but; accepting help from the man who bears that name does do something.

The name Iesous represents God's love for the world. Believing and accepting that love is what makes a person acceptable to God. John made many statements concerning love. Here is one of those statements. **Love is from God. Every person loving is born of God and knows God. A person not loving does not know God because God is love.** It is not a name but the one with the name that constitutes a relationship with another person. Many people receive gifts from someone they don't know but the sender knows them. The sender sees them as someone who touched his heart. This is what God does for people who touch his heart; he sends them his love. God does not offer them his love because of their knowledge or zeal. If love was produced by an act of love, everyone would love God or people who love them. There is no logical reason for the existence of love. It just is.

Billions of people don't know the name Jesus or Iesous. Does that mean they can't be acceptable to God? That would mean a lack of knowledge would condemn them. Christ said ignorance would not prevail against a direct communication from him. If God personally offers his love to a person who has never heard the name Jesus or Iesous, and that person accepts; God places a part of himself (love) in him. He may live his entire life without knowing the names Jesus or Iesous and be with God when he dies because he is a creature of love. Christ said, "All will be instructed by God." God goes to each person and tells him he loves him and wants to be in his life. It's the same thing a man does when he proposes to a woman. Loving God is not the same thing as knowing about God.

All kinds of evil live in people who espouse the name Jesus. They would be wise to understand, the name does not make them immune to a guilty verdict at their final trial. Misunderstanding the meaning of Peter's words, may cause a person to live a life of false hope because he is relying upon a name instead of the love represented by that name. Knowledge can't produce love. Love is a gift from God to those who will return it to him. It is the same with humans. One person may love another but he will only give his love if the other person will return it to him. One by-product of knowledge is arrogance. The arrogance of the Jews made them think God was helpless without them. Now the arrogance of well-educated church people and zealous Muslims think God can't save anyone without their help and their teachings. Ignorance only appears intelligent to a person who is ignorant.

ORIGINAL DAY THREE: THE TRINITY OF LIFE

1. The water, remaining after the separation, is scattered in the space. It is gathered into one place.
2. A part of this water was converted into something dry which came to be called land.
3. The dry and sea were confined to different places.
4. The firm (the dry) produced grass, herbs and trees which contained reproductive seed.

The original body of water was separated with a space between. One part was scattered in this space and God gathered it into one place. Once this was done he ordered the dry to appear. The word land is in italics (KJV) which means, there is no word "land". The word translated earth is the word for firm, which describes God converting liquid into a solid, referred to as "dry". Now the water and dry are one, approximately round, object.

The water, the firm (land) and the air are the three component parts of earth, making earth a trinity. At this time the land (dry) is in one piece and separate from the water. If Adam had not sinned, all people would have been able to live together in peace on one piece of land. There would have been no conflicting knowledge that would cause God to separate them. Sea is a symbol that represents people (Revelation 17:15). Here it is a picture of the separation of people.

The earth now consists of three things; air, water and soil. The soil is the lowest form of life and the source of the physical body and physical things. According to Christ the water represents the physical birth which includes a brain to care for the body. Air represents the breath of God (same word in Hebrew and Greek) which is the substance of a god who lives in a physical human body. (psucha-sue-k=breath, as in breath of life). This life form in a body is sometimes called "soul". The word grass has the meaning of something that sprouts. The word herb has the meaning of green. This includes grass but also many different kinds of plants. The trees are called fruit trees because they produce something that can be used for food by humans, animals, fowls and insects. On this third day; air, water and land became a paradise where man could live in this perfect trinity provided by God.

The plants had the color of green which became a metaphor for life. Green trees and plants have a therapeutic effect upon the psyche of humans and perhaps other forms of life. These green plants produce oxygen which is necessary for air breathing creatures. The grass is food for certain animals and contains medicinal ingredients that fight diseases. The herbs include green vegetables which was the first diet of humans and animals. Man began as a vegetarian but the more he reasoned with his brain, the more he convinced himself it was acceptable to eat the flesh of other living things.

All the creatures God formed from the ground and named by Adam were creatures that could give him companionship, comfort and happiness but not contentment. When man began using the creatures for food, they developed a natural fear of him. Some things that appear to be approved by God are tolerances of man's ignorant ways. This is seen when things tolerated by parents for small children are not tolerated when they become adults. Tolerance has a limit.

It is assumed, without evidence to support the theory, the coats of skins God made for Adam and Eve were from animals killed for that purpose. It is more plausible to believe, if God could make skins for animal bodies from dirt, he could make coats of skin without having to kill an animal. The theory the coats were made of skins of dead animals and, the theory the offering of Cain was rejected because it was not a sacrificed animal, are not verified by the text. These are assumptions not supported by textual evidence. The confusion concerning Cain's offering is caused by the word translated "respect". The Hebrew word shawaw means "to gaze at". God didn't reject Cain's offering; he didn't gaze at it. Incorrectly translating the word respect is an effort by translators to support a tradition.

Abel killed another living being. Just as people gaze at a dead body, God was gazing at Abel's offering. God did not need to gaze at Cain's offering if what he saw was acceptable. The reason for Cain's anger is not known. He may have been an animal lover who was angry with Abel for killing an animal. God asked him why he was angry. If he answered, it is not recorded. He told Cain if he did what he should do, he would be accepted. If his anger caused him to want to punish Abel for doing something he didn't like, sin was as near as his door. Cain's problem was not his offering, it was his anger caused by the offering of Abel. Right or wrong, Abel's offering was a matter between him and God. Cain needed to let God handle the problem if he was not pleased. No one has authority to judge the way another person expresses his faith to God.

A well-educated preacher, who was pastor of a church of mostly, well-educated people, was asked to speak at a mission where the members were former drunks, addicts and prostitutes. The pastor of the mission was this kind of convert. As the straight-laced pastor sat in the crowd waiting to speak, a man kept saying the words "dee dee dee deese". This was his way of speaking in tongues. The preacher became irritated by the constant chatter and thought some unkind thoughts about the man. Suddenly, God spoke to him: "You need to be quiet! That man may know more about worshipping me than you." Just like human relations are personal, worship of God is a matter between a person and God. There is no one-way-fits-all way to worship God.

Killing an animal for food was easier and quicker than working a crop and waiting for it to mature. Animals were killed to satisfy the desire for food. The desire for food is what initially caused the problem. This revealed the evil, self-centered nature of man. God later condoned this killing to show man the result of his sin. Not understanding this caused God to be seen as a cruel and merciless god. Reasoning with knowledge led to the killing of humans. While there is a similarity of the death of Christ to the sacrifice of the Passover Lamb, Christ was not a sacrifice. The Jews and Romans saw him as a criminal worthy of death. Paul's words "The one, who knew no sin, became sin for us, that we might, in him, become the righteousness of God"; is not correct. Christ was considered a sinner and died as a sinner in the eyes of his enemies but, he was not a sinner. He proved that in Gethsemane. He died with sinners, not as a sinner.

After the beatings, his body was a far cry from the perfection required of the Passover Lamb. The redemption for mankind was accomplished in Gethsemane when he refused to permit his brain to shut down his body. Unlike Adam, he maintained control of his brain. He did that by completely submitting his will to the will of God. According to Luke, he experienced a coronary thrombosis so severe; blood seeped through the pores of his skin and dropped upon the ground. That's when he overrode the authority of his brain over his body and subdued death. His body did not die until he gave it permission to die. His body was no longer under the authority of his brain. Once he completed his assignment, he permitted his body to die so he could continue his work as nonphysical truth.

As truth he would not speak to physical ears; he would speak to the god in human bodies who could recognize truth. In the form of truth he went to all who died before him, to tell them they had a second chance to make a choice. Then, he appeared in a physical form to speak to his followers who were wrestling with the mixed knowledge which caused confusion in their brains. After doing this for forty days, he spent ten days with Father God, after which, he returned as truth in his nonphysical form. Enabling people of different languages to understand one language demonstrated his ability to communicate with every person, regardless of their heritage.

The enemy of God and man is death. God, like man, accepts the fact of death but, like man, he is not pleased when a human dies. The physical body was designed to be immune to death. People, living more than 900 years without being sustained by the god in the body, suggests that. Israel was told by God to sacrifice lambs and other creatures for different reasons. This was done because the limited intelligence of the human brain needed something physical to help it understand truth. The many times they saw an innocent animal or fowl die for what they did, helped them understand what was required for their redemption. This also caused a callous to develop that desensitized their feelings about death.

The earth is a trinity of land, water and air. These not only represent the three parts of man but they also represent the three kinds of people who lived in the third millennial day. This was the first appearance of a human whose relationship with God was based upon faith instead of knowledge. For 2,000 years man's understanding of God was based upon knowledge passed on by Adam and his descendants. 2,000 years proved knowing about God is not the same as knowing God. The Scribes and Pharisees are prime examples of this. Abraham was the first person, since the rebellion of Adam and Eve, whose relationship with God was based upon trust instead of knowledge. He was alive at the beginning of the third millennial day

The trinity of the earth is similar to the trinity of God and Man. The trinity of God is: God, his breath and his word. The trinity of man is: man, his breath and his word. Written or spoken words are processed by the brain. When the words are accepted as truth, the brain is in a position to receive nonphysical communication which appears as thoughts. This allows Christ to speak directly to a person. If a person's information about a subject is not based upon truth, he has no standard by which to judge incoming information from Christ. The thought may be coming from Satan. The most important contribution made by the church system, is the encouragement given to people to learn the information in the Bible. Sacred writings of different religions contain much good information. The more a person learns, the easier it is to recognize the voice of God speaking truth.

MILLENNIAL DAY THREE:
2,000-3,000-(2,000 B. C.-1,000 B. C.)-
THE TRINITY OF LIFE

In addition to representing the trinity of God and man, the three parts of earth, formed on the third original day, represent the three kinds of people who live during any millennial day. Some are people whose morals and conduct represent the lowest form of life like that found in the soil. There is little difference in the conduct of these people and animals. The second level of life is represented by the water. These are people who respond with mental intelligence to some standard of morality. The third level is represented by the air. These are people who, by sharing God's love, are controlled by the heart of the person which is the god living in the body.

The highest form of life is represented by air. Air is a metaphor for God's breath which is the source and sustainer of all forms of life. The morals and conduct of this person are more in line with the ways of God. He is able to know and experience things beyond the capacity of his brain. As a being like God he can experience love, joy, peace and faith. His brain relies upon circumstances to produce like, happiness and confidence which are counterfeits of love, joy and faith. Living by faith, he doesn't do good to be rewarded and abstinence from bad conduct is not because of fear of punishment; it is because of his concept of what he is. He knows a just reward or punishment is administered by what he does or doesn't do.

2,000 years filled with bad experiences passed and man still preferred the imaginations of his brain to God's instructions. The destruction of all but eight people didn't seem to change man's disregard for what God told him. By the end of 300+ years after the flood, the people of the world had again turned away from the living God to idols produced by imaginations of their brains. The human brain relies upon information it collects from the outside world but its most destructive influence is from thoughts produced by its own desires and imaginations. The evil thoughts and imaginations are inspired by Satan's demons. It was because the imaginations of the people were constantly evil; the flood destroyed the surface life of the world.

In Babel, the people were unable to communicate, except with those who spoke the same language. The people scattered across the one piece of land already occupied by others. They left the region of Babel (gate of God) and settled on all parts of the land. When they were sufficiently scattered, the land was separated into pieces. With many miles of water barriers between them, they had no way of communicating with people who thought differently so, similarities in what they believed produced some degree of unity which produced many positive things. They not only began speaking different languages; they also acquired different skin colors and characteristics. Yet, they were all children of Shem, Ham and Japheth who lived 300+ years before them. The scattering from Babel happened in the second millennial day.

The Bible contains very little information about any group except those who remained in the land surrounding Babel. This came to be identified as "The Middle East". Now, 350 years after the flood that destroyed all but eight people, these people have again chosen to live according to the influence of their imaginations, families and friends. The people are again 100% anti-God except for one man. Abraham was born near the end of the second millennial day and lived 113 years in the third millennial day. (born 1948 and died 2113) (2052 B. C.-1887 B. C.). Abraham lived 58 years during the lifetime of Noah. The unbroken chain of communication now encompasses more than 2,000 years with links beginning with Adam (4000-3040 B. C), and continuing with Methuselah (3313-2344 B. C), Lamech (3126-2349 B. C.), Noah (2944-1994 B. C.) and Abraham (2052-1887 B. C.).

When the third millennial day began, there was one man who trusted God enough to do whatever God told him. God told Abraham to leave his home and family in Ur and go to a land he would show him. Typical of the response of the human brain to God's instructions, Abraham adjusted God's instructions and permitted his nephew Lot, to go with him. As it is with all adjustments of God's instructions, Lot became a problem for Abraham.

During the third millennial day, God tried to reach man through faith initiated through Abraham. With the destruction of Sodom and Gomorrah he let man see the irresistible force of nature when no one is controlling it. With 400 years of bondage in Egypt he let man see how helpless he can be in the hands of powerful, evil people. With laws given to Moses, he tried to teach man a way of life that would show him the difference in good and evil so he would stop destroying himself. With military might, beyond that of human ability, he tried to teach man what could be accomplished when people depend upon him for success. By speaking directly with Abraham, God showed man direct communication with him was more valuable than all the knowledge he could collect from any other source.

One popular and powerful religion that existed during the life of Abraham was the worship of an imaginary god named Ba'al. One of the ways the people tried to please this god was to sacrifice their firstborn son to him. God used this evil practice to let Abraham learn there was no limit to what he might ask him to do. Trust has no limit. When God told Abraham he would have a son, he told him many things this son would accomplish. After that son became a vibrant young man, God told Abraham to kill Him. With little understanding of God and another world, people did not understand physical death was not the end for a person who trusts God. For those who love God, it is the beginning of a new life. Just as the birth of a baby is the beginning of a life far greater than the life it had in its mother's womb, physical death, of a person who trusts God, is the transference of the god in the body into a life far greater than the life it had in his body. The human body is the womb of time for the god inside. Sadly, many are stillborn.

While deciding to obey God and kill his son, Abraham had to wrestle with thoughts of the many promises God had made concerning this son. Was this Satan telling him to do this? Did

God lie when he told him all the great things this son would accomplish? Was God asking him to act like a pagan? These and other painful thoughts were a great challenge to Abraham but faith in God provides courage and will power to do what God asks. Christ explained this challenge: **If someone wants to follow me, let him deny himself, pick up his cross each day and follow me. (Luke 9:23)**. A denying of self is the first and highest hurdle a person must clear to be able to face the tremendous challenges of following God in a world where so many people don't know him or don't like him. A question that puts a person's commitment to God to the test is, "What can God ask me to do that I would not be willing to do?"

The greatest test of commitment to God is not a willingness to do something good or great. The greatest test of faith is to be asked by God to do something opposite of what a person has learned about the goodness of God, especially if it will do irreparable harm to people he loves. Will God ask someone who wants to follow him, to do something evil? Abraham's willingness to obey God was put to the most severe test when God asked him to commit an evil act by sacrificing Isaac. According to Christ, a willingness to do whatever God asks is a prerequisite for understanding the words and ways of God. Commitment to God has no limit. In the moment of faith, nothing exists except God. The most important question is not "do I trust God"; the most important question is, "can God trust me".

If the average Christian should be asked by God to do something evil, he would rely upon the information he has learned from the Bible, the preacher, his peers and others to reason with his brain. He would consider the loss of reputation, status and friends. He would conclude, "That isn't God. God wouldn't ask me to do something like that." The arrogance of the human brain is such, it thinks it can know what God will or won't do and it will not hesitate to ignore or overrule the voice of God if it doesn't understand or agree.

Many people feel justified in refusing to do what God asks because they cannot verify his instructions with the information in their brains. Religious people rely upon their teachings for instructions from God. This is acceptable as long as God isn't giving direct instructions. Relying completely upon their brain permits them to accept or reject incoming information from God and makes their brain the authority for their decisions and conduct. This is why a believer in God feels no guilt in rejecting instructions of God if they are not compatible with what he knows. Believing in the existence of God is the product of common sense and religious teachings. Believing God requires knowing him well enough to recognize him when he speaks. Recognition does not exist for someone not known.

A person's faith is not tested by being willing to do something good for God. Faith is a willingness to do anything God asks even when the brain rebels because it contradicts the information it has about God. Because faith relies upon a person instead of knowledge, it effectively eliminates any rationale the brain can understand using knowledge. Faith has no need of knowledge because the basis for faith is a person. Faith puts a believer in a position of having nothing to rely upon for a decision except a willingness to do what God is asking him to do. Note-the word is ask not command. God never cancels a person's freedom to choose.

Trust is not produced by knowledge stored in the brain because knowledge can only produce confidence, using compatible information. A person can recognize the voice of God even if his body is dead. Lazarus's body was dead but he heard the voice of Christ, reentered his body and revived it. The god in the body is the only part of a human capable of trusting. The brain will try to convince a person, the voice of God is a thought produced by his brain, to be mingled with existing information, for a "reasoned" conclusion. Abraham knew the difference in the voice of God and a thought in his brain. If God instructed him to kill Isaac, that's what he would do. A brain made of dirt is like a computer; it can only function with acquired information. A god in a body has access to the intelligence of God to help him make decisions. This is verified by the words of Christ, **My sheep recognize my voice, I know them and they are following me.**

In millennial day three, God uses different means to get man to accept the better way of life he offered him. Knowledge of him failed to influence the people so he introduced faith into the world through Abraham. All but a few of the people of the world had again chosen to put their confidence in information collected in and produced by their brains. God selected Abraham and told him to leave his family and home. A person's greatest human influence, both positive and negative, is his family. What God would tell Abraham would not have impressed his family. This is verified by the words of Christ. **A prophet does not lack respect except in his native land and in his house. (Matthew 13:57.)**

Abraham left his home and family in Ur to go to a place where God could talk with him without interference from his family. He settled in a place near a city called "Sodom". Sodom was a city where the people had become more vile in their thoughts and conduct than animals. Young Lot, his nephew, saw an opportunity for prosperity in this city. He left his uncle and took his family and servants to Sodom. Homosexuality was the norm in Sodom and, in time, Lot's people embraced and/or adapted to Sodom's lifestyle. Adapting to evil increases the difficulty of responding to God's instructions.

Man likes to make God responsible for everything in this world, including the forces of nature which God placed under man's authority. The respect nature has for man's authority over it is comparable to the respect man has for God's authority over him. Nature can only be controlled with the authority of faith. On one occasions the rotation of the earth was stopped and another time the rotation changed directions and moved backwards. This was accomplished by two different men. The desire to satisfy self caused the people to lose any concept of faith or its power. Like a loving parent protecting an undeserving child, God had held the reins of nature to keep it from destroying the people of Sodom and Gomorrah the way it destroyed the people with a flood.

As seen in the conversation with Abraham and his visitors; only a few righteous people are required for God to restrain the forces of nature. If God had not restrained nature, Sodom would have been destroyed long before it was. Because Christ revealed God more clearly than he had ever been revealed; it is obvious, by observing the words and ways of Christ, God is a protector not a destroyer.

This enables a reader of the Old Testament to understand God did not destroy Sodom and its people. Their love for evil destroyed their respect for God which prevented them having the faith required to control nature. It was when the people of Sodom reached a point of a reprobate brain that God took his hand of restraint off nature and nature, their subject, destroyed them.

The people to whom God chose to grant the gift of faith spent 400 years of the third millennial day in bondage under the rule of someone who didn't know God. God selected this group of people who had no concept of freedom, self-will, achievement or God. They were like a blank and crumpled sheet of paper. God began by showing everyone he was not another religious idea concocted by a human brain. He demonstrated his power to debunk the ten most popular gods worshipped by the Egyptians and reverenced by many of the Hebrews in bondage. Then, to demonstrate his authority over any part of the earth, he parted the waters of the Red Sea for the Hebrews and released them when the Egyptians started across. When their masters were no longer a threat, he led them to a place where there were no provisions to sustain life except him.

Being humans guided by their brains, it was natural for them to think they were going to starve. God spent forty years trying to prove to them he could be trusted. He provided his word (what-manna) in the mornings for their souls, quail in the evenings for their bodies and water from a rock for their thirst. Many naysayers in the group had to be killed to prevent an infection of unbelief of the whole group. There are examples that illustrate, God will kill to protect his own. A loving parent, willing to be killed for other reasons, will kill to protect his own. That's a natural instinct for a loving parent with the character of God. Trust is something that has a person or God as its reason for existing. The brain can use compatible information to produce confidence but it can't trust because there is too much conflict in its information. Confidence is produced by an agreement of compatible information. Faith is produced by trust for a person or God.

Faith does not require information because it relies upon the trustworthiness of a person. A consensus of the information related to a subject is required before the brain can produce confidence. The success of confidence depends upon the ability of the person. Confidence is always controlled by the brain. To train the brain to have confidence in God and fellowman, God introduced a system of moral standards for thought and conduct compatible with his ways. These moral standards were different from those learned from the deceiving lies of Satan and the idol worshipping people of Egypt.

To do this, he chose a Hebrew who became a favorite son of Pharaoh, a killer pursued by Pharaoh, a sheepherder in Midian, a dependable man with whom God spoke as one man speaks to another, a miracle worker, a leader of weak, ignorant, childlike people and a mouthpiece for the invisible God. God gave Moses the details of the history of man from the moment time began to the time of his life when he was about eighty years of age. This was about 1361 B. C. Moses's brother and most trusted confident betrayed him. Moses saw how quickly and easily people, who witness miraculous powers of God, can walk away from God because of the influence of others.

God's plan for these people was to inform and discipline their brains to stop acting like slaves or animals and learn to act like gods created in the likeness of God. With the brain harnessed, the god living in the body could more easily respond to God by the medium of faith. Contrary to his first instruction, God provided something physical to represent him. In addition to the pillar of fire and cloud which followed them, he had them make an Ark and a tabernacle (tent) for the Ark. For more than 300 years during the third millennial day this Ark represented God. The child-like people could see the Ark and things God did that were related to the Ark but, they did not have sufficient faith to see God. They could only see what God did. This permitted them to receive some knowledge of God but, as it is with all knowledge, their circumstances kept overcoming their confidence produced by their knowledge.

They had confidence in God based upon what they could see and hear but they did not have faith in a god that could be seen and heard without the use of eyes and ears. They had confidence in the symbol they could see that represented God but they didn't have faith in God. The symbol replaced God. Many Christians do not appear to recognize; objects like the Bible, a cross, a church building or some human that represents God, subtlety becomes a replacement for God. This is the reason God's ten instructions (commandments) forbade making anything physical to represent him. A true relationship with God is monogamous without any human or physical attachments. The pure love of a man and woman for each other is a physical parallel to the love of God and a human. Nothing else is needed or wanted.

ORIGINAL DAY FOUR: A COMPASS FOR MAN

The function of lights in the lofty (the space between earth and the outer water)
1. Separate the day from the night
2. They will be signs (a flag, a beacon, evidence)
3. They will be for seasons (a fixed time)
4. They will be for days (to be hot)
5. They will be for years (a whole age)
6. God made a greater light to rule the day
7. God made a lesser light to rule the night.
8. God made the stars (an illumined, hilly object)

Some think these first seven days were eons of time. When thought is energized with faith, thought and reality are instantly the same. Time is not required for something to be done. What God did on the fourth day destroys the theory the creation days were eons of time. The sun and moon were made to rule the day and night and be an instrument to regulate the amount of time in days, seasons and years. God did this in one day. If days four through seven were approximately twenty four hours of time and, the end of the first three days was described the same way, circumstantial evidence would render a verdict, all seven days were the same. A day (day/night) is a period of time about four minutes less than twenty four hours.

Light was created on the first day so, what appears to be lights in space are objects energized by the light created on the first day. A light bulb is not a light it is an object that can be energized to produce light. Electricity is an energy which can cause the filaments of a light bulb to illuminate. It is invisible but its presence is recognized when it illuminates or energizes something. The source of all light is the words of God, "Let there be light." Without those words there would be no light in this world or universe. Because Christ was/is the word of God, he is the source of the light of the world. He said, both he and believers are the light of the world. (Matthew 5:14; John 8:12).

Because light enables the eye to transfer information to the brain, it is a metaphor for intelligence. Like a compass, it lets a person see where he is and the direction to take to get where he wants to go. Christ said the light for the body is the eye. God separated the light from darkness on the first day. On the fourth day he placed objects in the space between the earth and outer water to reveal and reflect that light. The moon is a reflector of light emanating from the sun. The sun is not reflector of light but an object energized by the existing light. Like the wind, the presence of light is not known until it makes contact with a physical object. Both light and wind are metaphors for the substance of God.

God separated light from darkness on the first day and separated the water with a space on the second day. If astrologers should ever see past this space, which now contains innumerable, lighted objects, they would see the water that was originally joined to the earth. The statement, "He also made the stars," indicates the stars are not the same as other objects of light in space. The word for star is "an illumined, hilly object". The uneven surface may be the reason for the twinkling of the light. Some people think the sun is a star. The text indicates the objects in space, the stars, the sun and the moon are different. (1:14-16).

A sign can be something written on a board or, a symbol like the American flag. The American National Anthem contains the words, "the rockets' red glare, the bombs bursting in air, gave proof through the night that our flag was still there." No matter how dark the night may be and no matter how many people become casualties of doubt, a person only has to look upwards at the incomprehensible space filled with lighted objects to know God is still alive and well. All he has promised man is still intact and available. The word "signs" indicates the light reflecting objects, the stars, the sun and the moon all work together to reveal God. As the Psalmist said, **The Heavens record the splendor of God and the space reveals the work of his hands. (Psalm 19:1)**

It is obvious the sun acts as a sign of the beginning or ending of a day. It was special made and set at a proper distance from the earth so it could warm the earth without consuming it with its tremendous heat. To have different seasons the earth must rotate with changing positions that move away from, or back to, the center position a little each day. This was not caused by a catastrophe as some surmise; it was the way God designed it during this first week of time. How else would people in certain parts of the earth be able to enjoy the freshness of spring, the warmth of summer, the colors of fall and the beautiful snow of winter?

The sun not only acts as a sign of the beginning and ending of a day, it also acts as a warning for people who place love for self above love for God. Anything physical, that comes in contact with the sun, with a core temperature of some 27,000,000 degrees Fahrenheit, would not last a second. According to Christ, there is a nonphysical lake of fire which does the same to a person who leaves his body without the shield of love to protect him. The word translated brimstone, and thought to be sulfur, is the Greek word theion which is a form of the word theos (god). In Deuteronomy and Hebrews, God is referred to as a consuming fire. (Dt.4:24; 9:3; Hebrews 12:29). Brimstone represents the divine nature of God which, like the sun, cannot be approached without special protection. After a person's body dies, to approach God without the protection of love, means instant death.

God is the zenith of knowledge to which man is attracted. Go back to the beginning of this book and read again the incident of the insects. They landed on the sand and crawled toward the fire until the heat consumed them. The light of the fire was to the insects what the light of knowledge is to man. The insects were so focused upon reaching the source of the light they ignored the heat that killed them. People can become so focused upon the light of knowledge they fail to distinguish between good and evil knowledge and become a casualty like the insects.

MILLENNIAL DAY FOUR:
4,000-5,000-(1,000 B. C.-0)
A COMPASS FOR MAN

God put lights in space to act as signs of seasons, days and years. They also act as a clock to tell time and a compass to let people know where they are. They were put in place before the sun and moon were made. The sun and moon were made for special needs of the earth and its people. In addition to providing light, the objects are signs for life on earth. For instance, the relationship of the sun and moon are parallels to the relationship of God and man.

Because the route of the moon around the earth is a few degrees different from the earth's orbit, the size of the reflection of the sun on the moon is in constant change. The moon is almost always seen from the dark side of the earth. Whether it is a small crescent or a full moon, it lets the people, who can't see the sun, know the sun is shining. In the same way people who say they know God but rely upon religious systems for guidance, are in constant change as to how much of God they reflect. Christ said believers are the light of the world.

Sometimes, so much of the world is between God and a person, very little of God reflects off him. It is the same with the total population of the world. If history and current news reports are reasonably correct, speech and conduct indicate unbelievers so outnumber believers there is only a small remnant who reflect God. For instance, the changes in the moon from crescent to full, then back to crescent, represented the waxing and waning of the nation of Israel during the fourth millennial day.

It represents the strong and weak times of trusting God. Perhaps, most important of all, the only time the moon is totally eclipsed and completely dark is when it gets directly in line with, and between the earth and sun. It becomes dark because it blocks the view of the sun. Everyone, especially religious leaders, should see this as a sign of what happens when a person tries to be a mediator between man and God. They not only stop reflecting the light of God, they also keep people from seeing God. They have nothing to contribute except their own ignorance which is a metaphor for darkness. This is the meaning of hades which is incorrectly translated using the made-up word "hell".

Catholics, permitting the Pope to stand between them and God is one reason many of them have such a dim view of the reality of God. Protestantism, duplicating the church system of Catholicism with a business-like organization, has done the same. Judaism and Islam experience similar problems. There is very little reflection of God in any of them because they use God as a commodity to promote their agendas. Like the tree of knowledge, they produce some good fruit and an abundance of evil fruit.

For a little more than 300 years the people who followed Moses out of Egypt, fought and killed to claim land God gave Abraham. They were guided by warriors, judges and prophets who tried to keep some semblance of respect for God. It was a time when every man did what he thought was right (judges 17:6). God always seemed to have a prophet on hand, to echo his voice to the people but, the people ignored or killed them. When the fourth millennial day began, David was the king. There were twelve families (tribes) of Israelites who occupied different parts of the land God gave Abraham and one tribe that served as priests. This Promised Land was about one half of the original land of Eden. They were destined for failure because they were controlled by the emotions of their brains which kept interpreting or adjusting the words of God. As Israel prepared to wage war against the inhabitants of the land, God instructed every human and all animals be killed. Thinking only of time and not eternity, the human brain sees this as instructions of a cruel god like Satan, instead of God. Yet, they understand, if a physician intends curing a person of cancer, he must remove all the cancer.

If Israel was to represent God, they had to clean the land of all life related to its pagan inhabitants. This was an act of mercy for those inhabitants. By killing innocent children, those children would be without sin and qualified to live in Heaven. If they were permitted to live, even with the teachings of Israel about God, many would never see past their heritage. They would be remnants of the cancer of paganism that would destroy them and Israel.

This would enable Satan to use the people who were spared, who had been serving him, to influence the Israelites in ways opposed to God. This is what happened when Balaam told Balak what to do to defeat Israel. When good and evil mingle, evil will usually become dominant. Paul paraphrased the prophet Isaiah with the words, **The Lord says, "Come out from among them and be separate and don't touch that which is unclean and I will favorably receive you, be a father to you and you will be to me, sons and daughters."**

There are many Jews, Muslims and Christians whose allegiance to God is defeated by others whose lives are influenced by people serving Satan. All religions have a mixture of good and evil people. Most are guided by leaders and teachings and only a few have sufficient faith to rely solely upon God for guidance. God is that silent voice speaking to the god residing in the body, sometimes thought to be a person's conscious. Like Babel, there is confusion, and only a thin crescent of light to reflect the light of God. The fact the Jews were in bondage to Rome and killed their Messiah, after 1,300 years of being guided by instructions given them by God, are examples of what knowledge can do.

It was not David that made Israel great; it was following the instructions of God which, like the light reflecting map in space, showed the people the route to a Godly life. This fourth millennial day would let man see the impossibility of acquiring peace or solving problems by depending upon knowledge, even when the knowledge was good knowledge from God. Israel had the most accurate knowledge about God known to man. They had God's instructions for every phase of human life. Beginning with the powerful reign of David, these chosen people had 1,000 years to see what human effort guided by good knowledge would do. They would have 1,000 years to see if the map, given them by God, would be used to find peace and Godliness. Their decisions to adjust God's map to accommodate mirages in their brains produced defeat and bondage.

God's instructions reflected the light (intelligence) of God the way the countless objects in space reflect the intelligence of God. But, like the North Star and big dipper, a light only reveals where a person is, it does not compel him to go in any direction. Every prophet God sent to help the people know truth was rejected and/or killed. Each generation could see the faults of their fathers but could not see their own faults. Christ quoted the Scribes and Pharisees who said, **"If we were in the days of our fathers we would not have joined with them in the blood-letting of the prophets."** Then Christ said, **"You are your own witness that you are the sons of the ones killing the prophets. You are exactly like your fathers. (Matthew 23:30-31).** This is an example of history repeating itself.

David knew God's instructions to not commit adultery and not kill but he did both. He was the primary influence for God's instructions but didn't follow the instructions God gave him. Solomon, David's illegitimate son, became king and his addiction to sex has never been equaled by another. These are examples of God trying to do something with weak humans. God will use whatever he can get from a person. If everything about any person is known, no one would be a worthy helper for God.

Millions of people have health problems or some disability but their employer accepts whatever they can contribute. Wounded soldiers don't stop fighting because of their wounds. God is not looking for ability, he supplies that; God is looking for availability. After a demon gets a person to do wrong, he tells him he is not worthy to do anything for God. He tells him to stop trying so he won't look like a fool or hypocrite. Many people, who may look like fools and hypocrites, continue giving what they have to God. God wouldn't have anyone working with him if being worthy was a requirement. The only requirement is having the stubbornness and grit to be willing.

It is obvious God has sufficient intelligence to say what he means and mean what he says. Don't kill doesn't need an interpretation. Love your enemies doesn't need an interpretation. Interpretations occur when circumstances present a cost too great to apply the instructions or, someone thinks he has a better idea. Interpretations permit a person to replace the instructions with an adjustment based upon his opinion. If he thinks his opinion produces a better solution than the instructions, eventually the original instructions are replaced with interpretations or opinions of the instructions. This was a major problem for Peter and the church system which claimed him as their first pope. Repeated over time, these opinions became traditions with more influence over people than the original instructions of God.

Instead of going to the Torah for instructions, Jews go to the Talmud for an interpretation of the instructions. Instead of going to the Quran for instructions, Muslims go to the Tafsir for an interpretation of the instructions. Instead of going to the Torah and the words of Christ for instructions, Christians go to Peter, Paul and their church traditions for an interpretation of God's instructions. People in these three religions, whose faith roots go back to Abraham, are often deceived by their leaders who teach interpretations and traditions instead of the original information.

David's brain stimulated his sex drive and caused him to make the wife of a soldier serving under him, pregnant. Instead of being a man of God, confessing his sin and taking his punishment, he put out a contract on the husband of the woman and had him killed. David's conduct didn't fit the description of a man after God's own heart (1 Samuel 13:14). His illegitimate son became king over Israel and set a record for sex perversion never equaled by another man.

His 700 wives and 300 additional sex partners (concubines) all needed their own places to live and, these were not in the lower income part of town. He justified his robbery of the citizens of their money and goods, to feed his desires, by calling it a "tax". That warped thinking can be found in a decision made by the congress and Supreme Court of America. Outwardly, Israel was known as God's people but inwardly they worshipped their desires and ambitions. They had an abundance of knowledge about God but remained ignorant of the reality of God.

Israel experienced 400 years of bondage in Egypt with people who didn't respect or love them, telling them what to do. Then, they spent forty years in a barren land with someone who loved them telling them what to do. God's purpose was to move them from obeying because of force and fear to obeying because of appreciation and trust. Later, the prophets tried to teach them about God. The people grew tired of accepting personal responsibility based upon things the prophets told them. They wanted some person to be responsible for their circumstances and needs. They chose Saul because his size impressed them. When the brain needs to make a choice, it looks for outer appearances upon which to base its decision. This enables an unqualified and/or evil person to be chosen. The history of America records many politicians who were not qualified to represent others.

The reign of David produced a partial cessation of conflict by becoming the most powerful force in the area. Solomon, acclaimed as a wise man, is an example of how stupid a smart man can be. Israel was the only light in this world for God. David's evil conduct and Solomon's debauchery set the stage for rebellion. The ten Northern tribes rebelled against Solomon's son, Rehoboam, and began intermarrying with the Samaritans. About 722 B. C. the ten northern tribes of Israel were enslaved by the Assyrians. In 586 B.C., Nebuchadnezzar, of Babylon, conquered the two Southern tribes and all of Israel was again in bondage. When Israel's leaders moved between the people and God, there was an eclipse of God and Israel was in total darkness.

In the fourth millennial day Israel was like the revolutions of the earth which constantly changed the amount of God reflected in their speech and conduct. Sometimes, like a full moon, she reflected the brilliance of God. At other times, darkness enveloped her and, like the distant lights in space, memories of things God had done guided her as she walked in the dim light of despair. People, who aren't experiencing the reality of God, talk about things God did or something they think he might do. This is what a person hears from many religious leaders. Talking about what God did is old news. Talking about what God will do is opinionated hope. Talking about what he is doing is what people need to hear. This is what Christ instructed his people to do just before he ascended.

During Israel's darkest nights, the prophets, like stars in the sky, reminded her of God. Like the phases of the moon, there were times when Israel was the light for a world in darkness and other times when there was little light reflected from God. In spite of all of God's efforts to help the millions of people born into the world, only a few, a remnant, accept his offer. Yet, the world has always been filled with people worshipping something they accept as their god. False gods, produced by knowledge and adjustments of what God says, are expressions of self.

The desire of the brain is for itself and its body. The brain may manufacture an idea or agenda and become so committed to it; it becomes a physical or mental god. Today, the number has reached billions of people who practice some kind of religious thought and/ or activity contrary to the instructions provided by Moses and Christ. Is their action based upon a relationship with God who is a living being like them or, something their brain devised in its search for something to worship it could control?

Knowledge of the information in the bible can improve a person's speech and conduct but it does not make him a worshipper of God. This was proven by the Scribes and Pharisees who led in the crucifixion of Christ and many religious leaders who ape demons. The fourth millennial day ended in the blackest of darkness. Israel's leaders became the mediators between God and man and caused an eclipse of God. Just as the moon becomes black when it gets between the earth and the sun, Israel, the reflector of God, became black and put out the light of Christ, the only light of this world. The number four represents the physical earth. The earth now has an abundance of knowledge but is void of intelligence.

Original Day Five:
The Birth of Grace

1. Let the waters bring forth swarms of living creatures.
2. Let the waters bring forth fowl that fly above the earth in space.
3. God created the whales and every moving, living thing, abundantly produced by the waters.
4. These products of the water were instructed to reproduce.

It appears both the physical and nonphysical parts of creatures produced with water were created during day five but, the statement fowls came from the water is clarified by 2:19 where fowls are included in the formation of physical bodies from the ground. God made bodies from dirt for air breathing creatures after he made a body for man. This was after the first seven original days. (Genesis 2:18-20).

On this fifth day of creation, God produced bodies for water creatures but he only used the water to create the nonphysical part of air breathing creatures. The earth was filled with creatures without physical bodies. Except for the creatures of the sea, the earth was similar to the nonphysical realm where life forms have no physical body. Before God made a body for Adam, none of the creatures had a physical body. It was nonphysical life, living in a physical world. This is not difficult to understand for the person who understands Satan and his demons are nonphysical forms of life that live in this physical world. Water life is special in that none were on board the Ark and there is no record of any being destroyed by the flood. However, fossils found in different land areas indicate some died during the time water covered the earth or were left behind when the waters receded.

The creation of man and land creatures was not physical. Just as the male/female man did not have a physical body until sometime after the first seven days when plant life needed physical attention (Genesis 2:5), physical bodies for other air-breathing creatures were made after a body was made for man. It was the male/female who lived in the same body that gave names to the creatures. There are two worlds. The nonphysical world is like a mirror reflection of the physical world. A reflection in a mirror is not physical but it is still seen. This is like the vision provided by faith.

The creatures God created on day five were gifts for man. They would help him do his work, be a companion for him and entertain him. They were gifts of grace or, something extra, created for man's benefit. They remained faithful to their purpose through the centuries of time. Man doesn't deserve their devotion and that's what makes them gifts of grace. The world did not deserve Christ, the greatest of all gifts of grace. The demeaning treatment he received was much like that received by animals. The treatment of Christ, at the beginning of millennial day five, was the most despicable of all evil acts of man, in the first 4,000 years of time. For God to continue trying to help man, after they killed the body he inhabited, was the greatest of all demonstrations of grace.

MILLINNEAL DAY FIVE: 5,000-6,000-(0-1,000 A. D.) THE BIRTH OF GRACE.

The number five represents grace. A short definition of grace is "unmerited favor". Millennial day five began the greatest demonstration of God's grace which began with the birth of Christ. Normally, a male and female who join to produce an offspring will contribute to both the physical and nonphysical makeup of their offspring. The baby then has both, a male and female make-up like God and each of his parents. The physical body God made for the first man was only a physical dwelling for the god who already existed. God used tiny particles of dirt (dust) to make the first body which he called Adam. These dust particles became the cells of Adam's body. In the same way; God used tiny cells of Mary's body made of dirt, to form a body for Christ who already existed.

The manna in the wilderness was called manna but it was a physical form of God's word. In the same way, the body of Christ was called Iesous (whose help is YHWH) but, it was also a physical form of God's word. Otherwise, the instructions of Christ that believers had to eat his flesh and drink his blood would represent paganism. The manna was something physical; produced by God that represented his word. The body that came from Mary was something physical; produced by God; that represented his word. Because both were produced by God, they were vehicles used to convey the word of God which must be consumed to sustain life for a god living in a human body. This symbolism is further explained at the last supper when Christ said the wine and bread were his body and blood.

As it was with the first man, both the male and female parts of Christ came from God. Mary's only contribution was providing material for the physical body. She contributed the same thing the earth contributed when God made the body for Adam. Mary was to Christ what the earth was to Adam. Some religions call earth "mother earth" the way Catholics call Mary "Mother Mary". This leads to deifying the earth and Mary who had nothing to do with the creation of Adam or Christ. The earth and Mary provided the material God used to form a physical dwelling for Adam and Christ. Idolizing a human body indicates a lack of understanding of what man and God are.

God produced the body of Christ the same way he produced the first man. He used particles of dirt (cells) from Mary's body, made of dirt, to form the physical body of Christ. In the same way the male/female parts of the first man existed before the body was made, it was the same with Christ. Christ was the breath of God and existed before he was placed in a human body. The material from Mary's body only supplied the physical body. Mary made no contribution to the male/female parts of Christ. God said, "Let us make man in our image and likeness." Both Adam and Christ received their male/female makeup from God. Both were created by God who is both male and female. If calling Mary "The Mother of God" is valid, then the earth should be called "The Mother of God". God has no mother. The idea is ludicrous.

This is one of many examples how man's brain, a physical instrument, used mixed knowledge to distort the words and deeds of Christ during the fifth millennial day. Peter still had his problem of adjusting the instructions of Christ. He kept thinking with his brain instead of trusting what Christ told him. Even after he was reunited with Christ, after he denied him, Christ had to rebuke him for trying to interfere with his purpose for John. The attitude of Peter is seen in many people who trust their opinions more the instructions of Christ. They protect their opinions by refusing to learn or accept existing information. Just before he ascended, Christ gave instructions to the apostles and others to share what they knew about him, as they went about their daily activity. It is natural for a person to share his interests as he talks with other people in the common course of a day.

Peter, reasoning again with his brain instead of trusting what Christ told him, ignored what Christ told him. Because Christ wasn't there to correct him, he made the worst error ever made by someone professing to be a Christian. He established a church system patterned after the legalistic, synagogue system. What he did became the primary opponent of the plan of Christ to share the message of redemption with the people of the world. Christ's instructions to the people were; "As you are engaged in normal and natural conversations, share what I taught you by immersing them in the name (singular) of the father, son and holy breath." All three are known by one name. That one name was recorded by John and verified by Christ. **He was clothed in a garment immersed in blood and his name has always been THE WORD OF GOD. (Revelation 19:13).** John said God's word existed when the beginning began.

Physical immersion is performed in water, but the immersion of which Christ is speaking, is performed in the Word of God. Just as a physical, water immersion is a public demonstration of commitment to the agenda of a church; a mental immersion in the word of God is a public demonstration of commitment to God. Physical immersion is a one-time act witnessed by a few people. Immersion in God's word is a continuous act, witnessed by many people observing how a person's attitude and conduct are affected by God's word that was and is, Christ.

Instead of sharing what the Word of God (father, son and holy breath) had done for them, Peter and Paul mixed the teachings of Judaism with the teachings of Christ. When Peter murdered the man and his wife, he was enforcing the teachings of Judaism. People who professed Christ became sales people for their opinions, teachings and agendas. Christ's plan was to have all sheep follow one shepherd. The contribution made by a witness is pointing, by speech and conduct, toward the shepherd, so anyone interested will know where to find him.

Peter had spent his life in a synagogue system where human leaders were the teachers of information about God. The arrogance of these educated teachers made them think a person not taught by their teachers could not know about God. Christ was a mystery to the Jews. **The Jews were amazed and asked, "How can this man know what is written having never been taught?" (John 7:15).** As he had done on other occasions, Peter acted according to what he thought instead of acting on what Christ said. He and Paul promoted the synagogue system which used different levels of human leadership to teach information and enforce rules not taught or endorsed by Christ. Peter forgot or ignored the statement of Christ that everyone will be taught by God.

Peter's desire to be the spokesman for Christ led him to gather the believers in Jerusalem into an organized group so he could tell them what they needed to know and do. This demonstrates the ongoing conflict between knowledge and faith. He first told everyone to sell all they had so everyone could share equally. He appeared to think if no one had a personal ownership of anything, they would be equal. People are not equal. There are many differences in people. This idea of communion is the source of the idea of Communism. Sharing is approved by God providing it is done without obligation or force. It is the concept of a family where all share equally. Peter could now be the leader he wasn't able to be when Christ was present. He became the judge and executioner of any who did not obey his rules.

He, a leading representative of the Savior, became a murderer over money. If that wasn't bad enough; he said Christ, the breath of God, was the one who killed the man and his wife. A normal boss would have fired Peter on the spot but, as in so many cases, God has to work with what he has. If he fired a person because of a bad decision, he wouldn't have anyone working for him.

Paul considered himself an educated, sincere, dedicated and zealous servant of God. As a champion of Judaism he had no tolerance for anyone who thought differently from Jews. To him, a non-Jew was an infidel who needed to be subdued or killed. The only thing Christ did for him, when he was on his way to Damascus to persecute followers of Christ, was to let him know who he was persecuting. He did not replace his legalistic, Jewish thinking with the teachings of Christ. He only re-studied his Jewish theology. Was it his high opinion of what he had learned about God that kept him from going to, what he considered uneducated fishermen, to learn what Christ had taught them?

He demonstrated what is common among educated religious people. "That person who hasn't learned the scriptures through normal educational means can't possibly know as much as I know about God." This is what the educated Jews thought about Christ and the same attitude the well-educated Paul had about the apostles. After talking with Peter and James he said they didn't tell him anything he didn't already know. Was the information he learned from Gamaliel and others more accurate than the information the apostles learned from Christ? Many diamonds of truth are found by people digging out of holes of hard times that are not found in theological books and lectures.

A lover of truth listens with unbiased attention to everyone because he understands he does not know all truth. If his knowledge is based upon truth, it does not need protection or defending. That is how he learns of, and overcomes, errors in his information. He is grateful to any person who uses truth to show him a flaw in his thinking. After Paul went to Peter and James, he wasn't impressed with them so he began preaching his Jewish theology with an adjustment for Christ being the messiah. Because he was well schooled in the law and prophets, much of what he taught about God was in line with what Christ taught but, like Peter, he didn't understand Christ did not need something like a synagogue system to instruct his people. Paul was an organization man who didn't understand the shepherd concept of Christ. However, he did understand salvation was only available because of what Christ did.

Satan has an advantage over God in that humans respond to existing knowledge in the brain easier than the voice of Christ speaking directly to the god in the body. In less than sixty years the plan of God to save man by individual sharing was in shambles. Instead of a guerrilla type, natural sharing of information in casual conversations, Peter made the believers a conspicuous group of people. In doing this he put a bullseye on the Christians for the Jews and Roman government to easily see. This made it easy to persecute any who espoused the cause of Christ. Just before Christ ascended he told those present he would be with them to the end of their lifespan. The Greek word aionas means life or lifespan. Aionios means something without beginning or end (eternity-forever). The KJV translators did not make this distinction which is necessary for understanding what Christ said.

There came to be so many errors and distortions about Christ; about 90 A. D. Christ showed John the evil and corrupt ways of people in the church system, the domineering cruelty of government and the greed of people in commerce. He gave John a "state of the world message" entitled "The Apocalypse of Iesous Christ". Apocalypse means "a revealing". Preachers who teach the Apocalypse as an end-time message of calamity make it useless for people.

There continued to be so much disagreement about Christ and what he said, a little more than 200 years later, Constantine, the Roman Emperor, called a conference of religious leaders to reach an agreement about the information concerning Christ. By observing the changes in America over the past 200 years, the reader can get an idea how much the beliefs of people can change. It is reported, Constantine saw a sign of a cross above the sun with the Greek words, "en touto nika" which means "by this conquer". A curious question is; why would a Roman, whose native language is Latin, be given a message in Greek? If it had been in Latin it would have been "en hoc signo vince".

The Jewish people, who said they represented God, joined with the Roman government to crucify Christ. Now, those who say they represent Christ, join with the Roman government to determine the most accurate information about Christ. The first union produced the savior and the second union produced the Bible. Some important knowledge of good was salvaged out of this mixture of good and evil knowledge. Occasionally, God will use the ideas and efforts of less-than-acceptable people to produce something that benefits everyone.

They agreed to accept thirty eight Old Testament writings and twenty seven other writings which were called the New Testament. The authors of the New Testament writings had to be an apostle or someone who was personally acquainted with an apostle. These writings became the accepted teachings of the church system. There were many other writings by different people which contained truths not contained in the accepted writings. While it is important to learn the history and other information recorded in the accepted writings, it is more important to remember, God was speaking directly to people before there were any writings. Written information may appease the brain but it is not the same as direct communication from God.

The religious leaders met and made their decision concerning the many writings about Christ. Matthew, John, Peter and James were apostles. Paul was acquainted with at least two of the apostles and stated he was an apostle since Christ had commissioned him on the road to Damascus. Mark was acquainted with Peter and Paul. Luke was acquainted with Paul. The writing entitled "Hebrews" was included because it was thought to be a writing of Paul and did not contain contradicting information like that of Thomas, Mary Magdalene and others. There were many differences of opinion but finally the leaders agreed on what is called "The New Testament".

The greatness of the value of the Bible is beyond estimation. Its purpose and value have been diminished by people who treat it as a holy object and rely upon interpretations of its information more than the meanings of the words when first spoken. King James translators were influenced by traditions to give false translations of some words and transliterate other words which, if translated, would expose errors in traditions. The value is also lessened when people take the word of a leader instead of personally reading the text with a willingness to do what Christ, God's Breath of Truth, reveals to them. Christ said, as the breath of truth, he would remind of what he had said and then lead to complete truth. He can't remind a person of something never heard or learned.

With Peter, Paul, the Gnostics and others as teachers, it is little wonder people attracted to Christ were confused about what Christ wanted them to know and do. Because Christ speaks to each person according to his personal needs, what he tells one may be different from what he tells another. Confusion is produced when a person goes by what Christ told another person instead of going to him for personal needs. He can do this as an individual but, if he is a member of a group, what Christ tells him will be influenced by the opinion of the group. Information Christ gives to a person should be seen as evidence God will help those who seek his help. It should not be accepted as something he should use as a basis for future decisions because circumstances may be different. Rigid compliance with existing information is what caused Peter and Paul to teach and do things contrary to Christ.

About fifty four years after he returned as God's Breath of Truth, Christ met with John, now in his seventies, and showed him the condition of a world still relying upon knowledge instead of him. He revealed (the meaning of the word "apocalypse") to John the corruption in the church system, the domineering brutality of government and the unbridled greed of people in commerce. These three worldly systems operate as pyramid systems (600-60-6). 666 is not the correct way to record the three numbers. Satan uses religious teachings, government laws and desires for material possessions to control most of the people of the world.

The church system was called "Catholic". Catholic means universal. Its meetings, with its pomp and rituals, are based upon the synagogue system promoted by Peter and Paul. This government styled church system had a leader (6), a lower level of leaders (60) and the people (600). Titles like pope, bishop, clergy, pastor, deacon, etc. designated the level of authority of each office. This organized system, controlled by men, was a far cry from the instructions Christ gave just before he ascended. For the last 700 years of the fifth millennial day, the leaders of the church system replaced God with their teachings the same way the Jewish leaders replaced him with their teachings. Instead of Christ's message, "The reign of God has arrived," the message was, "The reign of the church has arrived." If Christ had appeared again in a physical body, he would have been treated worse by those who bore his name than he was by the Jews.

In 570 A. D. a baby was born and given the name, Muhammad. When he was six, his mother died, leaving him an orphan. When he was 25, he married a rich widow. When he was 40, God began giving him information to improve his life and the lives of others. He recorded the information and called it Quran. His teaching, "God is one", was a reaction to the church system teaching there was three gods. One was the Father; one was the son and one was the Holy Spirit. This permitted them to put Mary in the mix as the mother of the son part of the trinity. Through the centuries until modern times, preachers look foolish trying to explain how three is one. This is the first question a Jew or Muslim asks a Christian. The absence of a logical answer makes anything else a Christian might say, useless. The correct answer is obvious.

The result of God speaking to a human is often puzzling. It would seem if someone, like God, told a human what he wanted him to do, that human would do as God instructed him. Observing Adam, Abraham, Moses, David, Solomon, Peter and Muhammad reveals a tendency to always adjust God's instructions to accommodate a personal opinion or agenda. Many religious leaders, who begin with a sincere desire to help God help people, end up promoting personal agendas. The longer a person walks a tangent to truth, the farther he moves away from Christ.

Just as Peter adjusted the instructions of Christ to accommodate what he wanted, Muhammad did the same. About ten years after God began giving him this knowledge of good, he went the way of evil knowledge and began robbing caravans, killing people and taking their possessions. The information in the Quran indicates his knowledge was a mixture of Judaism and Christianity and similar to what the church system teaches. This mixture of knowledge can produce some evil results as seen in Muslims and Christians.

Now there are three different groups who say they represent God. The Jews, church people and Muslims; all saying they loved God; hated each other. The words of John tell the truth about all three groups. **If someone says, "I love God" and hates his brother, he is a liar. The person who does not love his brother who he sees is not able to love God who he does not see. (John 4:20).** Because of the emotion associated with conflicting, religious knowledge, religion is a major instigator of hate and conflict. It makes people in another religion appear inferior.

Grace has been defined as "unmerited favor". With that definition in mind, start at the beginning to see how much grace God has bestowed on the human race. He made man a carbon copy of himself. He gave this man a perfect place to live. He made this man and his descendants rulers over all the earth. He told man what to do, to forever enjoy these blessings. Man chose to make decisions produced by his brain instead of instructions from God.

Man's appetite can be one of his worst enemies. The desire for food cost Eve all the perfect gifts God gave her. Was this stupidity on the part of one person or is it seen in every person? The desire of the flesh for food, sex and mind altering drinks and drugs has destroyed God's plan for many people. Yet, in spite of this, God's love for man keeps him trying to show man the path to life. That is the definition and demonstration of grace.

Of all the previous times in history when God's grace tolerated the unworthiness of the people he loved, the fifth millennial day demonstrated the greatest demand on God's grace. In the years when admitting Christ was the Messiah meant imprisonment, torture and death, the remnant who knew Christ, saw death like an Olympic athlete sees a gold medal. Now, with both the government and church promoting Christ, admitting Christ was the Messiah was the popular thing to do. At no other time was more darnel (black kernel wheat) sown among the good wheat. Satan had finally turned Peter's misguided idea into a goldmine for his agenda. He could generate so much confusion, few would ever find truth. Now a church system, ruled by wicked people, could do whatever Satan inspired its leaders to do and make them believe they were doing God's will.

The remnant must have been very small during these centuries when the Catholic Church ruled the land. God would not permit Sodom to be destroyed if ten righteous people could be found living in Sodom. Of the millions living in the world during the fifth millennial day, the fact God didn't obliterate the whole mess was because there was always a few people who knew God as a real being, living inside them. The more a person looks at the attitude of man toward God, the more he is amazed at the unmitigated grace of God. Except for God's grace, not a single person would receive a revival of life. Just as Judaism corrupted the Torah and the messages of the prophets, the church system corrupted the message of Christ and zealots in Islam corrupted the message God gave to Muhammad.

The last 400 years of the fifth millennial day saw killing and mayhem by the people who said they were doing God's will. The evil precedent set by Peter was still alive and well. Like the Scribes and Pharisees, they were sincere in what they believed but, sincerity is not a substitute for truth. Good intentions have no value without good deeds. Through all of this religious chaos, God always had a few who put him above all the false teachings, rituals and killings of the religious crowd. Christ died for all but all but a few rejected him.

What happens when sincerity becomes a substitute for truth? What happens when someone is persuaded by a person who is sincere? If a sincere Jew persuades someone; that person is told to become a member of a synagogue so he can be told what to believe about God. If a sincere Muslim persuades someone; that person is told to become a member of a Mosque so he can be told what to believe about God (Allah). If a sincere Christian persuades someone; that person is told to become a member of a church so he can be told what to believe about God. All are sincere but, would any one of the three accept the teachings which the other two call truth because they are sincere?

Evangelizing people with teachings produces converts mentally confident what they learn is truth. Is truth determined by what one group teaches? There is no contradiction in truth. Christ said he, not people, was truth and would lead people to truth. When Christ leads a person to truth, what that person finds is not knowledge but love. Love is the only force strong enough to control conflicting knowledge. Malice and conflict exists within the ranks of Judaism, Islam and Christianity because leaders use a mixture of truth and lies to produce confidence in their brand of knowledge. As long as people trust knowledge instead of God, there will be conflict.

Teachings of Christ, that a person with faith could heal the sick and cast out demons, were often explained away to protect some leader's reputation because he was too proud to admit he didn't have faith to do these things. Christ's message "The Reign of God has arrived" was replaced with a telling and retelling of the information about Christ. The focus changed from individuals helping people in need to enlisting people to grow a church so the church could help people in need. Humbling of self was replaced with zeal to be conspicuous for God.

Instead of following Christ's instructions to pray in private, in a private place; prayer was done by the leaders and people in public places and became a required formality before meals and meetings. Instead of talking to God and waiting for his response, prayers were mini sermons with no response from God. Writings, which came to be the New Testament, were not available to the people because the church leaders didn't believe God was able to have something written simple enough for an ordinary person to understand. A preacher or priest was needed to explain, not what God said, but what he meant. This is the same thing people are taught about the need for a lawyer. Truth ceases being a simple statement of fact.

By observing the conduct of lawyers, dating all the way back to Christ, their goal is not to present truth but to prove another is not telling the truth. This is seen in the words of Christ. (Matthew 22:35; Luke 7:30; 10:25-29; 11:45-54: 14:3). No one can create more conflict using information than lawyers. The more they complicate information, the more time is required to reach a verdict and the more money they make. Their strategy provides them with power and wealth. They invented the art of speaking out of both sides of their mouth. Their practice of concealing or distorting truth to win a case illustrates their willful ignorance of or indifference to Christ's words, "All liars will have their place in the Lake of fire".

During the fifth millennial day three groups, who had revelations from God, sufficient to know about him, were the Jews, the followers of Muhammad and the people in the church system. The Jews preferred their traditions to what God told Moses. The people in the church system preferred their traditions to the teachings of Christ. The followers of Muhammad preferred their traditions to what God told Muhammad. No one was willing to listen to anything that challenged their traditions. All qualified to be abandoned by God but grace keeps God using whatever a person offers until death closes the door on his opportunity to return God's love.

Christ introduced faith to the world and demonstrated how faith could raise the dead, heal the sick and cast out devils (deceivers) which plagued people's bodies and brains. In addition to moving a mountain, Christ said there was nothing a person with faith could not do. When leaders in the church system could not exercise this faith with its invisible power, their pride caused them to begin teaching faith was only available in the time of Christ. They began to identify confidence, produced by the brain, as faith. They used confidence in information as proof a person had faith in God. This resulted in countless millions of people becoming members of synagogues, mosques and churches who had no relationship with the living God. Religion, not God reigned supreme

The mission of Christ was to show how faith could connect a human to God and enable God to reign in that human on earth, the way he reigns in the citizens of heaven. The authority enabling a person to reign was not rules or laws but love. The reigning was not over others but over self. A person who loves does not need rules or laws. Paul agrees: **Love does not mistreat another person. Love fulfills the needs of law. (Romans13:10).** The reigning was to be done by the god living in the human body, which is the heart of a person. Heart refers to the core or life source of a person. That god would control his physical brain with truth and his brain would choose conduct like that which exists in heaven. God, as love, would reign on earth and conflicting knowledge would be sifted through love to remove the clumps.

He began with twelve ignorant, ordinary men whose knowledge of God was what their religious leaders had told them. They knew of the law that came with a penalty applied by others for the lawbreaker. Christ taught them they were free to choose and the reward or penalty of a choice was not applied by God or others but by the consequences of the choice. The losses incurred by Adam and Eve will always be examples of lost potential caused by a bad choice.

How the brain responds to the instructions of the god living in the body determines the thoughts and conduct of a person. The god in the body may be evil like the demons thrown out of Heaven with Satan. God speaks directly to everyone living in a human body. The first requirement is to recognize the voice, as the voice of God. The second requirement is to choose what that voice is saying over the knowledge stored in the brain or the voice of a demon.

Even if the knowledge is something God said that's recorded in the Bible; a current statement by God to a person takes precedent over what that person has previously learned about God. Truth is "what is". There is no memory of the past or theory about the future involved. To properly deal with a situation, a person must only deal with current facts, which is the substance of truth. Christ is truth. A person does not have to like what God tells him, to trust him. God may ask many things of a person, that person doesn't like. It's a scenario like that of a parent and child.

When people have embraced and lived by certain religious teachings for years, they are not easily convinced some of their religious teachings are not approved by God. After about 3 ½ years of hearing and seeing what Christ said and did, a majority of the Jewish leaders protected their teachings by crucifying Christ. The need for truth being verbally communicated to people was now the responsibility of the eleven apostles and a few people. Peter had some major defeats in his efforts to represent Christ and Paul was never able to embrace some teachings of Christ that were in conflict with his many years of study of Judaism. Because Peter reasoned with existing knowledge in his brain, he thought some of the ideas of Christ were wrong. Christ identified the challenging voice coming from Peter as the voice of Satan (Matthew 16:23).

After vowing to never forsake Christ, he denied him when he was in harm's way. Unwilling to follow the instructions of Christ, he organized a group and installed Socialism as the method of operation. This led to a man and his wife being murdered by him over money. Then, he again manifest the presence of Satan's influence over him and said God killed them (Luke 9:54-56). His method of spreading the Gospel took the reins out of the hands of Christ, God's Breath of Truth, and put them into the hands of men.

Paul met Christ but waited many years to go to the men who had learned from Christ. He, like Peter, adopted the method of the synagogue system which relied upon men instead of God for leadership. He reasoned with his brain and transferred the incorrect theory of the Jewish expectation of the Messiah to an incorrect theory of the return of Christ. If he had talked with John he would have discovered his error. The word "church" is a fabricated word that represents a group. The Greek word for chosen represents individuals. A church is guided by a leader and subleaders. It operates like the world systems of government and commerce which function with a pyramid organization. The Chosen act as individuals, following instructions given them by Christ as God's Breath of Truth; erroneously called "Holy Spirit". The same breath that turned a useless earth into a living thing is what turns a useless human into a son of God (Genesis 1:2).

Unable to demonstrate the power of faith, preachers, rabbis and other teachers use the text of their religious writings to teach history. While this may be beneficial in helping people have an acceptable code of conduct, it does not produce faith for a god living in a human body. The confidence of the brain must have physical help to heal the sick, cast out demons etc. Faith does not require physical help. Christ spent about 3 ½ years teaching and demonstrating the power of faith. Faith is produced by the spoken word of God communicated to the god in the body. The brain cannot possess or understand faith.

A minister memorized much of the information in the Bible in his zeal to acquire faith to free people from diseases and demonic forces. The disagreement of his male/female make-up always prevented him having a single thought required for faith. One part had confidence in the information in the Bible but when the need to exercise faith arose, the other part was reluctant for fear of failing. Before dawn one morning, while reading the Bible in a praying

83

position on the floor, he fell asleep. God appeared in a dream and showed him why he wasn't able to have faith. Immediately after that, the phone rang. He answered it and listened while a nurse of a hospital began telling him how strange her call might seem to him.

An elderly, Catholic lady, at the brink of death, had refused Last Rites. Instead, she wanted another kind of minister to visit her. Not knowing any ministers, this nurse, and other nurses on duty, decided to hold the large, city telephone directory upright on its spine and let it fall open. Then one of the nurses closed her eyes and touched the open directory with the point of a pencil. The nurse told the minister the point of the pencil was on his name. While explaining, the nurse kept apologizing to the minister for telling him such a weird story. The minister told her he understood and said he would be at the hospital within the hour.

Arriving, he was led to an elderly lady who appeared to be no more than skin and bones. He introduced himself and told her Christ had sent him to tell her she was not going to die. She appeared to understand but was too weak to respond except with a facial expression. He took her hand and thanked God for her healing. The next day, about 11 A. M. she came to mind. He called the hospital to check on her. The nurse, who had called him the day before, answered the phone. She told him the lady had been taken to another hospital and was probably already dead.

The minister went to that hospital where he found the lady in the emergency area with needles in several veins and a respirator forcing air in and out of her lungs. He stood puzzled. After a few minutes, he asked a doctor walking past him when she would be taken to a room. With an irritated tone the doctor replied, "She's not going to a room. She's been dead since she arrived this morning. We've been too busy to take the equipment off her and send her to the morgue."

The doctor left and the minister stood silent for a few moments and then spoke to God, "You told me she wasn't going to die. What happened?" God didn't answer. Experience had taught the minister, when God doesn't respond to a question already answered, the answer he gave, stands. God only has to speak once to a person who believes him. Without a different answer from God, the minister acted upon what God had told him. He placed his hand upon the forehead of the lady and said to her, "Mrs._____, the doctor told me you are dead, but God told me to tell you, you were not going to die. So, I'll be back tomorrow morning to visit you in your room." The next morning the minister sat by the bed of Mrs. _____, who was the picture of health. She didn't recognize him and he didn't tell her what God had told him to do.

Bringing someone back into a painful world may not be the best for them but, it taught the minister it is not the written word but the spoken word of God concerning a specific subject that generates faith. Learning the written information about God can produce confidence but, as Paul said, **Faith is from (produced by) hearing. The hearing is by the specific word of Christ. (Romans 10:17).** Both lego and rema mean "to speak". Rema is speaking to a specific meaning of something. This is what Paul experienced when Christ spoke to him on the road to Damascus. It took that to give him faith to change his belief about Christ.

There is a difference in confidence produced from learning, and faith. **"Faith is the foundation (reason for) of hope. It is proof of something that has been done. (Hebrews 11:1). I am confirming (amen) this to you; whoever says to this mountain, "Be picked up and thrown into the sea," and not have a divided thought in his heart but is believing what he is saying is happening; it will be his. For this reason I am telling you, all of the things for which you are praying and asking, believing you received them; they are yours." Christ- (Mark 11:23-24).**

The words "divided thought in the heart" are the key to understanding the requirement for faith. The KJV of what Christ said is: **Again, I say unto you, that if two of you shall agree on earth as touching anything that they shall ask, it shall be done for them of my father which is in heaven. For where two or three are gathered together in my name, there am I in the midst of them.** Millions of times two or more people have agreed in prayer for the health of someone without getting what they requested. Verse 20 is speaking of two or more people but verse 19 is speaking of the male and female parts of each human.

This is a literal translation. **Again, I am verifying to you; if two, out of you living on earth, will say the same thing, concerning all things accomplished, which they might ask; it will come to them from my father in the heavens because; it is not two or three gathered in my name. There, I am in the middle. (Matthew 18:19-20).** There is a difference in people meeting in the name of Christ and the two parts of one person accepting a request as already being honored while they are asking. That is the way faith works. If when the request is made, it must be accepted as something accomplished. If the thought is divided (uncertain), it is because the two parts within a person are not agreeing.

What can cause this certainty at the moment of asking? The answer is love. A woman is thoroughly convinced her husband loves her more than himself or anything else. His greatest joy is pleasing her. She wants something he is able to give her and is convinced it is hers before she asks for it. She knows the moment she asks, it is hers, because of her husband's desire to please her. This is the way faith works. There is no doubt God loves each person but that doesn't produce faith unless that person is convinced God loves him with unrestricted love. A child knows his parents love him. He asks a parent for something and is so convinced he will get his request he is upset and asks why if he is denied.

Males and females aren't designed to think alike. Their approach to something is usually different so, whatever they decide will often require a compromise. When a separate male and female are forced to compromise to obtain something they want, it is usually an outer, not an inner, agreement. Faith is produced by an inner male/female agreement which is produced by mutual love. Inner agreement, produced by love, will produce the faith to make the request exist. This has been done many times by people who love.

Christ told the people to love others the way they loved themselves. In the same way a physical male and female can produce one desire for something physical, the two parts of one person can do the same if, there is no divided thought. People of faith are people of love. Without love there is no faith. Faith takes place in the heart (the god living in the physical body). That means faith is produced by the two parts of one person. To get the two parts in one person to agree is possible. To get many people to agree, without anyone doubting (having a divided thought), is not possible.

The words and ways of God, as presented by Christ, became weaker as the church system grew in numbers. The message of Christ, **"I am the way, the truth and the life; no one has access to the Father except through me,"** was replaced with teachings, rituals and works. Leaders taught and the people came to believe, God would not accept anyone who was not a member of a church. The confusion caused by Peter, Paul and others was so great, Christ returned about 90 A. D. to let John see the cause of the problems of people. He began by revealing corruption in the church system. Then he revealed the cruel character of government using the four horses and horsemen as metaphors. Next he revealed the greed and vanity of people in commerce. These three manmade forces are used by Satan to control most of the people of every generation. Only a remnant follow Christ close enough to choose his ways over the ways of the world.

The unwillingness of people to follow the instructions of God had again taken control of most of the people of the world. Revelation was given to John in symbols so only those willing to do what God might ask of them, would understand the message. Christ said a willingness to unconditionally do anything God requests is a requirement for understanding what God is saying. God talks to everyone. An example of understanding truth revealed by God is when God told Peter who Christ was. Christ told Peter his brain (flesh and blood) did not reveal that truth to him; it was the Father who gave him that truth. People may accumulate volumes of knowledge but if their knowledge is not controlled by love it can be a barrier to faith.

To prevent people understanding the message in Revelation, Satan counters with preachers who think the people and creatures in Revelation are physical and the message is about the future.

They change Christ's message of "NOW" into something in the future. They even use the Greek word "apocalypse", the title of the message, as representing an end time calamity. During the first half of the fifth millennial day, the church system of Peter and Paul became so corrupt, a reasonably, truthful person didn't want any part of it.

Christians, who use the instructions contained in the Quran to kill or subdue unbelievers, as a reason to label Islam a horrible religion, should read the instructions given to Israel when they entered the Promised Land. Nothing in the Quran surpasses the cruelty of those instructions. In the ten instructions given to Moses, while Israel was in the wilderness, God instructed Israel they were not to kill but, in the conquest of the Land of Promise they were instructed to kill everyone, even children. God deals with people on the level of their intelligence and ability. What has to be done may be far from what he would do under better circumstances. A doctor, after examining a person, would like to send him home without any medication but, if he has a serious health problem, he does what is necessary to save the person's life.

Through the centuries wars have killed millions of small children. Most people see that as something evil but, from God's point of view, these small children were the only ones in the group qualified to reign with him in Heaven. Sometimes when Satan uses people to kill, he makes a terrible blunder. Inspiring evil people to kill makes it possible for the slain, small children to inherit eternal life. Like Adam, before he sinned, they are in a state of innocence. If they had been permitted to mature, they would have been evil like their parents and perished in the Lake of Fire.

God loves humans, especially those with a child-like nature. On one occasion, parents were bringing their children to Christ and the apostles were stopping them. **They brought to him infants so he could touch them. Seeing this, the disciples rebuked them. Iesous called them to him saying, "Bring the children who were coming to me and do not prevent them because, in these are the reign of God." (Luke18:16).** The unmotivated love and honesty found in children is what God looks for in adults.

According to Christ, God is Truth. If, when a child reaches a stage of responsible maturity, he rebels against what God tells him, he is rebelling against truth. Like Adam, he is reasoning with the knowledge in his brain instead of trusting what God is telling him. He loses the guidance of God in the same way Adam lost the guidance of God by choosing to trust knowledge. Knowing the love of God, this is not likely to happen until a child has lived several years. Trusting knowledge inevitably ends up trusting a lie. Because a lie is the archenemy of truth, a person who lies becomes an archenemy of God. He has joined ranks with Satan. Christ said Satan is the father of liars. God talks to children but unfortunately, the influence of parents and peers can cause them to refuse to do what God tells them to do.

The cultures and moral codes of different people are not barriers to God. When God identified Christ to Peter, Christ told the apostles the gates of ignorance (hades) do not prevail against the voice of God. Often truthful comments of children are repeats of something they heard inside. God speaks to each person, to give him the same chance he gave Adam, to confess his rebellion, apologize and let forgiveness change his attitude. A change of attitude is known as repentance. If what God did to provide forgiveness doesn't change a person's attitude toward him, the person will continue trusting the information in his brain which will cause him to fall short of the level of life required for citizens of Heaven. Just as certain life forms are not permitted to live with humans, certain gods are not permitted to live with God. Remember Satan and his followers? They were not permitted to live in Heaven.

In the last years of his life, Muhammad became wealthy and powerful. His resentment toward the Jews may have been caused by Abraham not giving the birthright to Ismael, his first born son and forefather of Muhammad. In the first part of the fifth millennial day, the Roman government had no mercy on those who professed being a follower of Christ. Then Constantine added Christianity to his collection of gods and had all the people baptized to be "saved". Large pits, usually used for dipping livestock, were filled with water and the people went through the water in droves. This filled the church system with people who knew little, if anything, about God. Fortunately, because of the individuality of human nature, some of those people qualified to receive God's gift of love.

The most important public event of the fifth millennial day was not the birth of Christ or the death of the human body occupied by Christ. The most important event was private. It occurred in Gethsemane when Christ subdued the authority of his brain which was programmed to stop the functions of his body when certain conditions were present. It was there he conquered the power of death by overriding the authority of his brain. In the book of Revelation, Christ identified this event and his crucifixion as Armageddon and called it "The Great Day of Almighty God". This was the "evening and morning" of the first day of God's new creation.

I saw, coming out of the mouth of the great serpent (Satan), out of the mouth of the small wild animal (religion) and out of the mouth of false prophets (religious leaders) three, unclean breath-like creatures that looked like frogs. These are god-like creatures going to the rulers of the whole inhabited earth, performing miraculous signs to prepare them for the war of the great day of Almighty God. Be alert; I am arriving like a thief. To be congratulated is the person paying attention and clothed so he won't be walking around naked with everyone seeing his shame. He (Satan) gathered them in a place called in Hebrew, "Harmageddon". Revelation16:13-16. The admonition, following the words "be alert" makes what happened to Christ in Gethsemane the challenge for every human of every generation. Victory belongs to those who pay strict attention to what is going on inside their head and who completely submit their will to the will (instructions) of God.

Satan marshalled all his human and non-human forces, to put enough pressure on Christ, to defeat him in his effort to remain master of his physical brain. The stress was so great, he experienced coronary thrombosis so severe; blood seeped through the pores of his skin and dropped upon the ground. His brain was the place where the battle was fought and the victory was won. By the time he reached the cross, the only thing left to do was sign the peace treaty between God and man. This peace treaty was signed with the blood of Christ. Paul wrote concerning this. (Ephesians-chapter two).

Adam lost because he didn't overcome the power of his brain. Christ won because he overcame the power of his brain. Through the centuries, Satan had accused man to God. (Job 1:9-11; 2:4-5). According to the Quran, Iblis (Lucifer) was jealous because God created another god who was a duplicate of himself. Satan's response was jealous anger which caused him to challenge God by accusing and discrediting man. A human, accusing other humans, is evidence of the inspiration of Satan. God decided he would become a propitiation for man. This would eliminate any legitimate charges Satan might levy against man. Satan gathered all his forces in Heaven and on earth to defeat the breath of God residing in the physical body of Christ. The only power that could defeat all these forces was a complete willingness to do the will of Father God. When a problem is too big to handle; submitting to the will of God and letting him handle it is the key to victory

This battle fought by Christ was similar to a court scene where Satan, representing himself as the defendant, brought an endless list of accusations against different people on earth as a way of being exonerated for his rebellion against God. It's the idea, if enough people are doing evil, instead of being punished for the evil; the rules are changed to avoid punishing the large mass of people. If enough people on earth are evil, God will have to change the rules or he won't have anyone in Heaven. Satan actually convinces some people of this stupidity.

Satan had reliable evidence to support his accusations because every person was a failure, like him. His desire and effort to hurt God, by hurting people he loved, was thwarted when God ruled he would be a stand-in for man. God did; God endured; God won. Case closed. Charges dismissed; the accused is free to go. Like the reaction of the fans when the home team scores the winning touchdown; the cheers broke out in heaven:

I heard a loud voice in heaven saying, "Salvation, power, the reign of our God and the authority of his Christ has arrived because the accuser who stood before God day and night accusing our brothers was forcefully overthrown. They overcame him by the blood of the lamb; by their words of witness and they did not love their souls (the life part or a human) until the time of death. Because of this, let the heavens and those dwelling there rejoice. Woe to the earth and sea because the deceiver has come down to you with great anger because he knows he only has a small amount of time." (Revelation 12:10-12).

The words, "did not love their souls until the time of death" is a way of saying their primary concern was not the wellbeing of their physical life. During the time of their life, until they died, their primary goal was to represent God, even if it meant physical death. They loved God with their heart (inner self), mind (mental ability) and might (physical ability). (Deuteronomy 6:4-5). Simply put, God is first in love, thought and conduct. Love for family makes it the greatest challenge to making God first but, if a person doesn't win this challenge, he will lose many other challenges of Satan. The answer to the following question reveals a person's determination to be wholly submissive to the will of God: "What can God ask me to do, that I would not be willing to do?" Anything but "nothing" is a failing answer.

In Daniel (10:13; 21; 12:1), Michael is the one who stands for the people of God. It was Michael who stood against Satan and defeated him. Paul and Jude are the only ones to use the word "archangel". Paul referred to Christ as an archangel in his misconceived return of Christ theory. All references point to Christ as the archangel who is referred to as Michael (one who is in the likeness of God) who defeated Satan and 1/3 of the population of heaven. Archangel is not a translation but a transliteration. Arch is a Greek word that means beginning or origin. Ayyelos (yy=ng) is a Greek word that means messenger. If translated, archangel means the original or chief messenger.

Christ was and is the primary messenger of God. He is God's breath (incorrectly translated spirit). Thoughts are translated by breath, using vocal chords. The message in the breath becomes words. That's why John called Christ, who is the breath of God; "The Word of God". Christ told the apostles he would return as the breath of truth. The vocal chords in Christ that converted his message into words are now in people who translate what he tells them into words to help others. He is truth speaking to every person. Accepting truth is accepting him.

It was his attitude to put the request (will) of God above his own that enabled him to defeat Satan. The defeated Satan and his followers were exiled to earth. In Heaven, before he was exiled, Satan accused man to God. This information can be found in the book of Job. Now, confined to earth, he angrily accuses God to man. Satan is a god similar to human gods but, unlike humans, he is not handicapped with a physical body and brain. Paul recognized man's battle is against beginning beings who are the lords of ignorance (darkness).

Christ reminded the Jews, "Man is a god". The Greek word translated demon means "divine" or "god". Satan and those exiled from heaven with him are gods. A human, handicapped by a body and brain filled with destructive desires and opinions; who thinks, without God's help, he can defeat a god who hates him and not handicapped by a body, is a fool. Every human generation has proven that.

A few, "a remnant", embrace the voice of God speaking inside and represent him as "as you are going, make disciples" witnesses. They don't think like the people in the religious pyramid systems (600-60-6-on forehead) and they don't rely upon the authority (600-60-6- on right hand) of the religious pyramid systems. They are partners with God. They share their knowledge of and experiences with God in the way they speak and live.

Their words and conduct attracts attention. Then God uses their words and conduct as an introduction to what he wants to tell the person. Converts are not counted because there is no way of knowing how the person to whom they witness responds to

God. The backsliding of many who make public professions of faith proves that. Many converts are people who are influenced to make some kind of physical response motivated by persuasion and emotion. That's why so many preachers tell an emotionally stimulating story near the end of their sermon. Emotional people are more vulnerable to tactics of persuasion. Christ is not revealed by words but by love. People who are a part of religious systems like Judaism, Islam and Christianity may represent their teachings and programs but, is love seen and felt in what they say and do?

During the fifth millennial day the church system had internal conflict between the leader in Greece and the leader in Rome. Both wanted to be top man for God. That sounds like what Lucifer wanted. The Roman leader won first seat and the Greek leader segregated his group from the Roman faction. God was not represented by the Jews, the church system or Islam but, there were a few of each who accepted God's proposal of love. Since the people were ordered or coerced to be identified with a religious group, all the people "belonged" to some religion. But, as Christ told the apostles, "I will establish my Chosen upon this rock and the barriers (gates) of ignorance (hades) will not prevail against them". That rock is God's willingness and ability to speak directly to a person the way he spoke to Peter. Nothing can destroy that rock.

Christ identified Peter as a petros (pebble). He said he would establish his chosen upon a petran (a huge unmovable rock). Paul referred to this rock (petran) as the one that supplied water in the wilderness journey and said it was Christ. **Everyone drank this breath beverage. They drank from the breath rock (petra) following them. That rock (petra) was Christ. (1 Corinthian 10:4).**

Five is the number for grace and it certainly took a lot of grace to die for people who didn't like him, work with people who wouldn't obey him and tolerate leaders who, like Lucifer, were wanna-bes of him. It was not easy to find enough cohesion in these particles of dust of the earth to form a body. As usual, God had to work with people more controlled by their brain than by him. They had adequate information but by the time their brains got through processing it, the conclusions contained many errors. A large circle of people playing the game of "gossip" is an example of how an original message can be distorted. Many errors were caused by scribes and translators adhering to traditional opinions. Peter's church system has always had people who trust the words and leadership of man more than the words and leadership of God.

By the end of millennial day five, the church system was filled with corrupt leaders and distorted and/or untrue teachings. The chosen were scattered in something comparable to the wilderness where God was the only provision and hope. Their goal was not to please a pope or abide by religious teachings; their goal was to listen for the voice of the shepherd and follow him. As Christ said, to do this a person must deny self, take up his cross and follow him. Someone made a statement appropriate for a person who chooses to follow Christ while living in a world controlled by Satan; *It is better to walk alone than with a crowd going the wrong way.*

ORIGINAL DAY SIX: THE CREATION OF A GOD, LIKE GOD

1. Let us make man
2. In our image
3. Like us
4. Let him have dominion over everything in the sea and on the earth.
5. God created man like himself.
6. He created them male and female.
7. God created a carbon copy of himself.

It is important to note the plural pronouns "us", "our" and "them" and the singular pronoun "him" in Genesis 1:26-28. The words "us", "our" and "them" represent more than one but "him" represents one. If this was speaking of physical bodies it would be impossible to understand. This isn't speaking of physical bodies because God doesn't have a physical body. It isn't speaking of God and another god because what God created was one god with male/female characteristics, who was a duplicate of him. If man was made like God and man is a male/female being; God is a male/female being. Confusion is caused by thinking of physical male and female bodies instead of one, nonphysical being like God.

The word for image is phantom or illusion. Christ identified this as "God's breath". Without breath nothing can live. Just as physical breath is necessary for physical life, God's breath is necessary for all life; physical and nonphysical. Losing access to God's breath is what caused Adam and Eve to die even though their bodies continued to live. Man was made a carbon copy of God. The word "like" represents shape or character. Wind is a physical likeness of

God. Wind and breath are the same word in Hebrew and Greek. The context determines which is to be used.

Man was created from the substance of God as a duplicate of God. He was a clone of God. God designed man to be his mate. Just as Eve's body was produced with a part of Adam's body to be a mate for Adam, nonphysical man was produced with a part of God, namely, his breath, to be a mate for God. Man was created equal to God. Equality is not determined by intelligence or ability, it is determined by love. Man's choice, for or against God is made as an equal; not as someone who needs to be bribed or coerced. A person who rejects God is not punished in a place traditionally called hell; he ceases to exist along with everything else in the realm of time. His penalty is the same as a rejection of a human proposal of love. The one who declines the offer is not punished by the suitor; he just forfeits what the suitor is offering. The word hell is a fabricated word. There is no Greek word that can be correctly translated using the word hell.

Since man is a duplicate of God, God can be understood to the degree a person understands self. If God is both male and female, one man or one woman is both male and female. The first physical body was not made until there was a need for someone physical to cut the grass, attend other vegetation and till the ground. (Genesis 2:5). After the first body was made, both male and female characters lived in that one physical body for an undetermined period of time before the second physical body was made. God planted the garden to be a home for him and this new god. Just as a human presents the best he or she can produce to impress a potential mate, God did the same. He created a spectacular universe as a residence for him and this god he wanted as his mate.

Observation of the way a physical male thinks and the way a physical female thinks; reveals they are different. Neither fully understands the other so, something has to be used to get them to agree without resentment. Christ said a house or a kingdom, divided against itself, cannot stand. What is true with a physical male and female is also true of the male/female nature in every person and God. If the difference in thinking can't be overcome, an agreement can't be reached? The only thing that can resolve differences without resentment is love. The character of God, who has a male and female identity, is love. Love enables the two different natures in God to operate as one without resentment of either part. This is necessary for him to have the power of faith. Inner disagreement (doubt) in a person is what prevents him having faith. This can produce low esteem and a fear of failure. Faith is an irresistible force that makes thought, instant reality. It also produces confidence for the brain.

Love, producing faith in God for a human, is similar to electricity manifesting itself in an object. Direct current flows in one direction and alternating current alternates from the object affected back to the source. Direct current represents the flow of God's love to all men. This one direction love does not produce faith for a person. Alternating current is the flow of God's love to a person who sends it back to God. This completes the circuit, producing faith that enables both, God and the person, to experience the joy of being loved which provides the energy needed to accomplish what is desired.

Differences are resolved by this love; enabling man to trust God without a need for mental understanding. Because love produces faith, faith is evidence of love. A parent experiences joy when doing good things for a child but, that joy is not as great as when the child, without any feeling of need or obligation, does good things for the parent. God has feelings just like a human. Courtesy and kindness toward God causes him to feel blessed.

If a male part of a person wants to make a decision and the female disagrees (manifest in the brain as doubt), mutual love will cancel the disagreement; permitting a decision to be made. When two humans love each other, a difference in thinking is resolved without resentment because each prefers granting the desire of the other more than getting something for self. When God asked Adam why he ate the fruit from the tree of knowledge, instead of showing love for Eve by accepting responsibility for what he did, he blamed Eve for his disobedience. He did not demonstrate love for Eve. This was the second evidence showing Adam had lost his faith because without love there is no faith.

People with low esteem are people whose male/female nature has become estranged. Like Adam and Eve, this will cause one part to blame the other for a bad decision. The two parts of a person have many disagreements about doing or not doing something. If the thing done turns out bad, there is the same sense of condemnation that is seen in Adam blaming Eve. If one part of a person does not have love to forgive the part of him that made the wrong choice, a condemning attitude will develop and interfere with efforts to agree for future decisions. This will cause anxiety when faced with a need for a decision.

If this happens often, animosity will develop between the two parts of a person which will negatively affect his ability to have confidence or faith. His self-image will become more and more negative and his belief in failure will grow larger than his belief for success. Just like Adam never forgave himself for losing everything because he listened to Eve, many people never forgive themselves for doing something stupid because they listened to the part of them that was giving bad advice. A bell can't be un-rung but it can be properly rung by the person who lives today instead of reliving yesterday.

Eve was emotionally moved by the words of the Serpent which silenced the warning God had given her. The female part of a person makes decisions based upon emotion produced by the reasoning of the brain. The brain is a conference room where options are discussed for a decision. The male is designed to use existing information to make decisions and the intuitive ability of the female causes her to rely upon her feelings to speculate for decisions. If the male part of a person is persuaded by the female part or, by a physical female, he will make a decision based upon hope or theory instead of reality. The beauty and ways of a female, both the one inside and the physical one outside, is difficult for a male to resist. The female is definitely not the weaker sex. When both parts of a person trust God, there is no disagreement.

This is the way both are designed. When the female part is persuading the male part, the will of the male to listen to and obey the voice of God, is challenged. The result is something neither wants. In physical males and females, if the wife dominates, the husband will relinquish his position of authority assigned him by God and begin to make decisions to please his wife. This is different from wanting to please her because he loves her. This eliminates the objective nature of the male and leads to mental decisions based upon emotion produced by selective knowledge instead of decisions based upon the words of God. This feminization of the male results in God-less decisions for a family, a community and a nation.

The 144,000 virgins mentioned in Revelation 14:1-5 represent people who did not allow an inner or outer partner to sway them from doing what God told them. They acted as an individual male or female inside the body and as an individual male or female when they were connected to a physical mate. No one could turn them away from God because, their love and commitment to God was stronger than all other loves and commitments. They are the people from all races and cultures who love God above all else.

The number twelve is mentioned many times in the Bible. Because the 144,000 represent the redeemed of God from all classes of people, the most logical meaning is determined by adding the number five, which represents grace and the number seven which represents completion. By doing this, twelve represents perfect or complete grace which is required for a human to be redeemed. Two twelves would not represent Israel (12 tribes) and Christians (12 apostles) because there were thirteen of each. The tribe of Levi were priests and Joseph was represented by two sons. Judas betrayed Christ, and Paul was commissioned when he discovered who Christ was.

It is more reasonable to think this is twelve square. 12 square = 144. When a number is squared, it reproduces itself a number of times equivalent to its value. This plan to reproduce self is what Christ told his followers to do. This is the way a physical population is produced. 144,000 represent God's perfect (7) grace (5) which causes one individual believer to reproduce himself to produce an innumerable host of people who are one family (1,000-Hebrew-elef). Elef represents people of the same family or cause. 12 x 12 x 1,000 =144,000. The number, 144,000, does not represent a number of people but a kind of people. They are the redeemed.

When God made a body for Eve, he separated the two and made each free to do whatever they chose to do. Because the male/female character they had when they occupied one body was separated, they were the only humans who were 100% male and 100% female. If they were to ever experience oneness again they would have to love each other more than self. There is no motive for love, it just is. It cannot be produced, controlled or destroyed. Although there is a male/female part in every human, except Adam and Eve, an offspring receives only a male part from the father and a female part from the mother. This enables an offspring to have both, a male and female character and be a duplicate of God and each parent.

Each child of Adam and Eve had a male part from Adam and a female part from Eve. Because the next generation had both male and female parts in each, the male contributed the male characteristic of his two parts and the female contributed the female characteristic of her two parts. The sex of the physical body determines which of the two characters is dominant. This produced authority, not over another person but over the second part in each person. The male was given authority over the female in a male body and the female was given authority over the male in a female body. How each relates to another person reveals the inner relationship. When a man acts like a woman and a woman acts like a man; Satan has succeeded in persuading that person to help him oppose God.

Satan can distort this law established by God by affecting speech and mannerisms and stimulating an unnatural desire for someone of the same sex. He gets his victims to reason with knowledge which produces emotion instead of honoring what God did. He mentally and physically distorts mannerisms of these victims the way he distorts mannerisms in other handicapped victims with mental and physical disorders. If medical science would learn how

Christ dealt with mental and physical disorders, many more people would be healed.

Satan used the natural traits of a woman to entice Eve with the fruit of the tree of knowledge and the natural traits of a man to entice Adam with Eve. He knows the weaknesses of men and women and uses that which enflames their desires and curiosities to cause them to look away from God. God told them if they ate the fruit from the tree of knowledge of good and evil they would die. He was not referring to their physical bodies; he was talking about them, the gods living in the bodies.

Just as air is necessary for the life of a physical body, God is the source of all life and necessary for life for a nonphysical god living in a physical body. Anything that separates a person from God separates that person from life. Not trusting causes a separation of man and God and man and man. Adam and Eve died when they stopped trusting God. The curse is not something God did to man; the curse came from ignoring the warning of God and eating the poison of conflicting knowledge. Conflicting knowledge is the primary killer of the human race. God does not hold someone responsible for the crime of another. A person is not deprived of life because of what Adam did; he is deprived of life when he does what Adam did.

When Satan told Eve she would not die, he was speaking of her physical body. When she ate the fruit and did not physically die, it appeared God had not told her the truth. Being physical, the brain can only reason with information that represents physical things. This is one of the ways Satan is able to lie without appearing to lie. He gets a person to mentally think of something physical that is a parallel of something that exists in a nonphysical form. Her physical body did not die but she, the god living in the body, became separated from God and no longer had breath necessary for life.

Proof of her death was seen in her insensitivity when she asked the only other person in the world to do what she did. People who accept Satan's offer of something destructive to them do not hesitate asking others to join them. It is the same with people who enjoy good things. This method, successfully used by Satan, is the method

Christ told his followers to use. Peter and Paul, programmed by the synagogue system, which was operated by laws and obligations, did not understand this.

Satan does not have to persuade people who have permitted evil to control them to talk and, God does not have to persuade people who enjoy fellowship with him to talk. They naturally share their experiences with others. A person persuading another to join him in evil, seldom feels guilty for the harm he causes the other person. A concern something they do may kill or destroy, does not affect a person with a conscious seared by sin. A person who tries to get another to join him in harmful activity is inspired by a demon. Evil finds comfort in numbers. Eventually the words, "everybody is doing it" convince the ignorant; doing and sharing evil is ok even if it challenges the authority of God. Anyone who continues to think it is wrong has some label placed upon them. What God says doesn't matter anymore.

Love died in the Garden. Now, without love there can be no agreement; without agreement there can be no faith; without faith there can be no relationship with God. (John 3:29). Love requires freedom of choice. Love is what Christ said about wind; no one knows the source of love or its destination. Love cannot be produced, controlled or destroyed. "Like" is a counterfeit of love. It is produced by words and conduct, and can be destroyed the same way. It can give shallow and temporary satisfaction but, like the body's desire for food, it has to be continually fed. Love produces contentment.

During the first seven days and, for a time after that, life on the surface of the earth existed without physical bodies. The bodyless male/female-created man was a duplicate of God who is not physical. They were one being without a physical body. Their means of communication was not with audible words produced by a mouth but with telepathic thoughts. The communication with creatures was the same. When life resides in a physical body, whether it is a word of a person or the bark of a dog, the language must be understand to transfer thoughts. Because thoughts are all one language, communication was natural among the creatures, creation, God and man. Thoughts were understood by everyone and everything. When God or Satan speaks to a person the words usually appear as thoughts, causing some people to assume they are produced by their brain.

The apostles heard words but the tree heard thoughts when Christ cursed it. Language is not a barrier when communicating with thoughts. This is seen when Christ returned on the day of Pentecost and people with different languages instantly understood one language because they were hearing the thoughts that produced the words. It is not uncommon to recognize the difference in the words a person is speaking and the thoughts he is thinking.

The words "man" and "Adam" are the same Hebrew word. The word means something that is flush or rosy in complexion. Since man is a duplicate of God, God is rosy in complexion.

The brain can't comprehend something that is not physical having a colored complexion. The male retained the name "man" or "Adam". Eve (life giver) is the name Adam gave to the female. One can only guess how long it was after the sixth day that God made one physical body for the two of them. This was when vegetation had grown to the point of needing physical attention (Genesis 2:5). The first body was occupied by both the male and female parts of man for an undetermined period of time.

God planted a Garden in the land of Eden (delight, pleasure). If the whole land of Eden was a paradise, imagine the beauty of the garden. Because everything could be accomplished with a thought, visiting different places in Eden or the vast universe, was instantaneous. In that garden two different trees would determine man's choice of God or knowledge. The tree of life represented God and the tree of knowledge represented the human brain.

Choosing the tree of life would make life simple. All they had to do was trust and do what God told them. The tree of knowledge of good and evil would complicate life. Not being omniscience like God, the brain would have to constantly guess which information would produce good and which information would produce evil. The choice between God and a human brain is comparable to choosing a pilot for a trip, who knows everything about flying an airplane or, choosing a pilot who read a book about flying an airplane. One, can pilot the plane through the storms of life and the other will crash.

Because Adam was separated from God, God told him he would have to spend the remainder of his life depending upon knowledge for his decisions. His brain, not God, would be the solver of his problems. During the seven days of creation and for a time after that, everything was done using the medium of faith. Faith is something that converts a thought into existence. Knowledge of what God does and says may be processed by the brain to produce confidence but, confidence requires a tool and time to perform; faith doesn't. The knowledge about God a person gets from reading the Bible may instill confidence which improves his life but, it is not the same as faith in God.

Trusting God produces unity and peace; trusting knowledge produces confusion and conflict. If there is only one center point, an unlimited number of circles can be drawn without a single conflict. Because accumulated knowledge is both, good and evil, there is no way to have one point of reference. The first conflict between Adam and Eve came after they decided to move from the one center point of what God said, to the many center points of knowledge. If a person doesn't trust what God says, he must rely upon his knowledge or the knowledge of others.

The three systems that use knowledge to control the people of the world are religion, government and commerce. Religion replaces God with teachings, government replaces God with laws and commerce replaces God with wealth. In all three, there is a mixture of good and evil knowledge which produces good and evil results. People, who use love (God) as their center point, will endure and often overcome the conflict caused by their mixture of knowledge.

Eve initiated the conflict between knowledge and faith when she chose to trust knowledge she acquired from the serpent. No matter how intelligent knowledge may appear, it cannot accomplish what faith can accomplish. To see the brilliance of Lucifer, think of the brilliance of things and ideas produced by the human brain. The brain is a magnificent, computer-like piece of equipment that collects information from many sources, including its own imagination, Satan and God. This information in the brain will agree with or oppose God when he speaks to a person. Because faith is trust in a person or God, it relies upon a person or God instead of information. The way Lucifer challenged God is parallel to the way a brain challenges the god living in a human body. Lucifer wanted to be like God, which is the way God created man.

God told Adam, since he trusted knowledge instead of him; he would spend the remainder of his life guided by knowledge instead of faith. Now his only hope is to use knowledge he learned about God to regulate his knowledge from other sources. The conduct of people through the centuries reveal the use of knowledge obtained from God and the use of knowledge obtained from this world. Knowledge can only produce what a person can do. Faith can produce what God can do. Like Adam and Eve, each person must choose knowledge or God as the principal authority for their life. New knowledge is impressive because it is compared with existing knowledge. It would appear retarded if compared with the knowledge of God.

Knowledge causes conflict because it has many sources, including the Bible. God provides truth for a person's needs. The chaos among people in the world in any century reveals the failure of knowledge to solve problems. Christ said a person who accepts responsibility for his sin (confesses) is deemed righteous (justified). Think what might have happened if Adam had confessed his sin instead of blaming Eve.

MILLENNIAL DAY SIX: 5,000-6,000-(1,000-2,000 A. D.)-THE CREATION OF A GOD-LIKE NATION

Millennial day six saw extreme birth pains before a parallel to the original day was born. In the sixth original day one man was created in the image of God. In the sixth millennial day one nation was created with the potential of being in the image of God. This nation was founded upon principles more closely aligned with the instructions of God, than any other nation in history. The words given to Israel through Moses and the prophets were like an introduction to the words and demonstrations of Christ. Israel was waiting for the arrival of their Messiah; America accepted Iesous as their Messiah. It is the only nation to be called a Christian nation. Out of the ignorance and ungodliness of the dark ages, a promised land immerged where people could be free to worship and work as they pleased. Freedom to choose is the foundation required for anyone who wants to become a mate for God. This freedom is not found in the rules of religion.

The sixth original day was the day God revealed his purpose for creation. He took a part of himself and created a duplicate of himself for the purpose of having someone his equal to love. Love can be painful if there is not another to share it. The love for family and friends gives much satisfaction and comfort but, no one can produce anything comparable to the contentment of mutual love of a man and woman. The sixth millennial day was the millennial day when God created a nation of people who had the freedom to share his love. They were different people with different ideas about God but they were free to make their own decisions.

This "land of the free" became known as "America". America, like Adam, was to be the object of God's love. He gave her everything her heart could desire but, like Adam, her knowledge that produced confidence in God was overcome by her knowledge that produced evil. Since the knowledge of different people is different, they must separate into groups that think the same way. Otherwise, they will end up like the people of Babel, collectively doing things harmful to all concerned. They did that to some degree with the formation of states but the idea of oneness prevailed and a civil war was the result.

Leaving her first love, her likeness of God became flawed and her light that reflected God was dimmed by her desires and ambitions. Like the people at Ephesus (Revelation 2:4) the people suffered many things and promoted the words and ways of God but without love, her dedication was defeated. Her respect for God, that made her the envy of the world, was overcome by her physical desires. Like Adam and Eve, she lost her respect for the words and ways of God. She could not resist the temptation to trust knowledge instead of God for her decisions. In time, knowledge replaced faith; religious teachings replaced God and love of self replaced love for others.

With knowledge provided by God, she became the most powerful and wealthy nation of all who went before her. Good knowledge, inspired by God, produced many innovations which benefitted the people but, the knowledge that produced success produced an arrogance that made God less and less needed. Money was able to fulfill so many needs it was desired more than God. God wasn't needed except in severe cases beyond the reach of money. Like Adam, America became so engrossed in things she wanted, she ignored the advice of God and the evil part of her knowledge overcame the good part. The desire for wealth permeated everything, including the church system. She boasted the biggest and best of everything including weapons to kill and destroy. Like Aaron; to please the people her leaders built her golden idols made of fame, fortune and power which permitted her to manipulate truth and do whatever her heart desired. Her relationship with God began to erode.

Instead of following the instructions of Christ to share with people in natural conversations, America, inspired by a misguided church system, set out to convert the world to her way of thinking about Christ. A plan, to evangelize all nations, changed her from a witness to a salesman and infected the government as it tried to convert other nations to its democratic form of government. Instead of being a wise fisherman who waits for the fish to come to the bait, she tried to push her religion and government upon other nations. Her interference in the affairs of others caused conflict with established religions and governments. Many people were helped but, eventually, her government became hated and her teachings about Christ became a religion, tolerated but not wanted by most of her own people.

Just as Constantine's misguided zeal for God filled the Catholic Church with unbelievers, the misguided zeal of evangelism filled American churches with people who were led to believe saying certain words was all that was necessary to be accepted by God. The wheat and darnel (black kernel wheat) grew in abundance... together. There was little difference in the conduct of believers and unbelievers. The human body, God's temple where he meets privately with a person, was replaced with buildings to accommodate crowds of people. The respect given these buildings made them fit the definition of idols. Like idol worshippers through the centuries, many church people saw their buildings as holy places. The degree of reverence paid a church building was comparable to the impressiveness of its architecture and extravagance of its building material.

To serve in or, better yet, to lead in the building of a large expensive church building gave special status to the leader. The fruit of the Tree of Knowledge of good and evil made a delicious meal. Pastors, ignoring what Christ said about the difficulty of a wealthy man entering the reign of God, became men of wealth. Because wealth was seen as the best way to get things done, wealthy people were especially welcomed by leaders and people in a church. Many said their wealth was God's way of blessing them. Some taught God could be bribed into giving a person success and wealth if he would send the preacher "seed money". This was an alternate version of the requirement to tithe one's income to be faithful to God. Obligation is a tenet of religion. As Satan told Christ, "Worship me, and I will give you all of this."

The miracles produced by God, which Israel saw In Egypt, the wilderness and the conquest of Canaan and, the times when their disobedience opened the door for their enemies to slay and capture them, did not make a lasting impression upon the Jews, Muslims or Christians. The brilliant human brain was handicapped by its arrogance when processing knowledge supplied by God. It was always in conflict with the god living in the body and any information it received from God.

It took more than 1000 years for the Jews to dismantle God's plan to use rules and laws to help the human brain understand the ways of God. This happened during the fourth millennial day. It took another 1,000 years for the people professing to be Christians to dismantle the plan of God, revealed in the words and ways of Christ. This happened in the fifth millennial day when the church system replaced God with teachings, rituals and human leaders. Using Old Testament instructions God gave to Israel, Muhammad used force to enroll followers and subdue Jews and Christians who he saw as enemies of God. This began in the fifth millennial day and continued throughout the sixth millennial day. During the sixth millennial day, Jews, Muslims and Christians were killing each other and many of their own people.

Christ told the seventy pairs he sent to the towns and villages to tell the people the reign of God had arrived. As previously stated, two represents one viable witness. For 2,000 years Christ led those who recognized his voice. For 2,000 years the human race saw the difference in people who trust knowledge and people who trust the words of God. After 2,000 years of witnessing what faith in Christ can do, America has arrived at the same place of Godless religion as Israel in their 2,000 years of being taught the words and ways of God. When knowledge is king, history will repeat itself.

During the sixth millennial day, to provide a way for the common man to know the history of God's efforts to save him, bibles were translated from original languages. The Bible became the number one best seller. Why then, did ignorance and confusion still reign among those professing they knew God? Why did Jewish people refuse to read information about God written by Jews? Why did Muslims zealots not learn the peace taught in the Quran doesn't come from conquest but from love for fellow man? Why did Christians not understand talking without doing made them hypocrites (pretender-actor)? Why did the people of the world not embrace the information that explained; God made man to have someone to love?

The answer is found by looking at something that happened in the garden in Eden. A human, loved by God, listened to a deceiver appealing to her brain which was too naïve to recognize a lie. Satan was jealous and hated God because God created someone who outranked him. He wanted to hurt God but God was too big to challenge so, instead, he attacked God's kids. Like a trusting child, Eve trusted him. Since then the choice has been to trust mixed and conflicting knowledge in the brain or trust what God says. The chaos in the world, in every generation, tells the choice made by most of the people.

The mixture of knowledge in a person's brain produces a mixture of good and evil. Peter and Paul did much Good but they are also responsible for much evil. For the remainder of the fifth millennial day and far into the sixth millennial day, the Catholic Church system ruled with an iron and evil hand. There was no resemblance to the words and ways of Christ. The translation of the Latin Vulgate permitted some, who wished to learn, to read what Christ said and did.

Because of the domination of the church system with its distorted teachings about becoming approved by God, more than half of the sixth millennial day passed without a clear message of how to become a son (offspring) of God. Because confidence in what was taught was confused with faith, many joined churches. Even though the King James Bible made it possible for the common man to learn about God, traditions were protected by the translators by using made-up words, words that didn't correctly translate the

Greek words and, transliterations. This prevented people knowing some of the most important teachings of Christ. Because of its great contribution, it eventually came to be considered by many to be perfect without any flaw. This was caused by an irrational understanding of Paul's words, "All scripture is given by the inspiration of God." While the word grapha may refer to the Old Testament writings which were called scripture, Paul could not have been referring to the writings in the New Testament because the New Testament wasn't complied until almost three hundred years later.

For instance, the words of Christ concerning the requirement of a new birth to qualify for Heaven were not translated correctly. Instead of translating anothen, "from above", it was translated "again" in John 3:3 but "from above" in John 3:31. Nicodemus, one of many leaders of the Jews, whose allegiance was to God, was also a teacher of information about God. He interpreted the statement of Christ about being born from above as another physical birth. This apparently influenced the King James Translators to think like Nicodemus and use the word "again" instead of the correct word "above". Again represents a repeat of something already done while "above" tells of a procedure where life on one level becomes life on a higher level. Life is not something physical. Life is a nonphysical entity that allows the physical body it inhabits to have the appearance of life. Christ asked him, "You are a teacher of Israel. Don't you understand these things?"

Things in time are patterns of things in the timeless realm. Life in soil is a lower form of life if compared to the life in a kernel of corn. If the kernel of corn is placed into the ground, it will draw the life in the soil to it. That life in the soil which responds will leave the soil and become a part of the kernel. That soil life is then born from a life on a higher level than the life of the soil. Being born from above, it is now the above kind of life of the kernel. This transformation of life that began in the soil can continue until it reaches the level of human life. The word "eternal" represents the kind of life, not the length of life. There is no time in Heaven. Christ said if he is lifted up from the earth, he will draw all men to him. His lifting up on the cross is a metaphor of his lifting up in the lives of people. It is his lifting up in the lives of people that draws all people to him. The cross is evidence; people are proof.

The kernel experiences metamorphosis and becomes a plant with a stalk, sheaves, tassel, cobs and finally, many kernels of corn like the original kernel that began the process. As Christ said on so many occasions, only the finished product is harvested, everything else is burned. Christ said this place of burning is the Lake of Fire which is the second death or the second time the god who lives in a human body, dies. Religious systems like Judaism, Islam and Christianity contain many people who are educated, sincere and dedicated, who are part of the plant, who do not have the love for God that makes them a duplicate of God. Their allegiance is not to a living God but to teachings, rituals and self. This makes them a candidate for the second death.

The first death is like that which happened in the garden when Adam acted upon the words of Eve instead of the words of God. A person, who reaches a time in life when he must choose God or his accumulated knowledge and, makes the same choice as Adam and Eve, will be separated from God and die. This is the first death. If he is born from above by accepting and returning God's love, he will be revived and not die a second death. If he is not born from above, as Christ told Nicodemus, he will not enter or even see the reign of God.

Children have the same immunity to death as Adam and Eve had before they sinned. If they die physically before they are mature enough to consciously rebel against God, they are acceptable to God when they leave their body. They don't experience any death. Immersion (mistranslated "baptism") has no effect upon a baby or adult. Some church leaders give people a false sense of security when they say being immersed and being a member of a church is proof they are a Christian. Others say church membership is necessary to become a Christian. Belonging to a church contributes nothing to the act of being born from above. Ask Nicodemus. He was a lifelong member of the synagogue and obeyed all its rules.

Only those who accept the love of God become a kernel. The rest are rebels or parts of the plant. Both are burned.

During the fifth millennial day God, through Christ, brought forth new life to the people of the world. The "be fruitful and multiply" instruction on the fifth original day is comparable to the instructions of Christ, "As you are going, make disciples." The physical multiplying was to be done by a man and woman. The multiplying of Christ is not done by a person and words about God but by a person and God. If God isn't in the mix, nothing happens. The original day instructions were matched by the instructions of Christ which instructed individuals to multiply by sharing what they knew about God. On the sixth original day God made a nonphysical being like himself which he called "man". On the sixth millennial day God selected people from different parts of the world who loved him and formed a physical body for them which was named "America".

By the time the sixth millennial day began, using the fear of going to hell to scare people or, promising Heaven to bribe people were popular sermons used to persuade people to become members of a church. Church was no longer just religion; it had become big business with many prosperous and wealthy preachers and priests. The Protestant churches were so much like the Catholic Church there was little reason for disagreement. The goal became finding something agreeable to use as a reason to get along with each other. God would surely understand if some of his instructions had to be altered or ignored for the sake of agreement.

Ignorance of God was as common as ever and, politics in the church system were as corrupt as politics in America's government. Evangelism replaced the "as you are going" instructions of Christ with successful evangelists becoming famous. This filled churches with a mixture of Christians and non-Christians which is described by Christ as the enemy sowing darnel among the wheat. Accumulation of many people and much wealth was considered evidence of faith in and blessings from, God.

Many good things are done by people in the church system which cause some of them to think this is proof God approves the church system. The Jews who crucified Christ thought the same thing. Acceptance by God is not determined by balancing good and evil conduct on the scale of righteousness defined by popular opinion. Many people, including Atheists, do good things from time-to-time. It is important to see how Christ measures the value of good works. Scribes who knew Scripture, Pharisees who zealously kept every detail of Scripture and Nicodemus who was an influential man of good character all fell short when it came to being acceptable to God. The one thing that makes a person acceptable to God is not good works but love, which produces a willingness to put God first in all areas of life.

Not everyone who says to me "Lord, Lord" will enter into the reign of Heaven; only those doing the will of my Father who is in the heavens. Many will say to me in that day, "Lord; Lord; did we not prophesy in your name and in your name cast out demons and do many works of power?" At that time I will agree with them *but reply,* **"I never knew you." (Matthew 7:21-23).** Many good deeds are done by people who openly reject the words and ways of God. These are as helpful to people as the good deeds done by people who know and love God. Doing good deeds is commendable but it is not the same as knowing God.

Giving to a needy person may not be what God wants done. That person may need to feel the pain of a bad decision before he gets relief, so he won't make the same bad decision again. Another person may need to feel the pain of a challenging situation to prepare him for a future assignment from God. The training required to play football is appropriate to illustrate this. The coach requires a player go to and endure the limits of his pain and ability in practice so he will be able to do the same when he faces the same kind of pain and challenge applied by an opponent. If one player tries to lessen the pain of a fellow player, he may be interfering with the plan of the coach to train that player. Like everything else in a person's life, good works need to fit the plan of God. The welfare system is proof of the great damage done to people when their needs are met without any effort from them.

In the last century of the sixth millennial day, a major attack on the people of America caused young and old to contribute something. Even young people helped by searching for metal that could be used to make armaments. Women worked alongside men in shipyards and other places to build weapons of defense. When this war was over, what women had experienced, caused many of them to realize they could be a breadwinner just like their husbands. They didn't seem to realize something worse than an enemy attack would happen if they left the assignment God gave them to teach and nurture children and teach young mothers the importance of the same. They began to find employment outside the home. A major decline in the character of children followed. Children left to themselves or someone hired to watch them cannot experience what a mother, who respects God, can give them. Sixty years later, young people, embracing a mixture of religion and worldliness, are blind to the meaning of "God first".

Some mothers with children and no husband are forced to be both, a breadwinner and a mother. Other women, seeking fame and fortune in the world of commerce and government, are part-time mothers. Each generation of children moved farther from God than the one before. Without knowledge of the information in the Bible, which records the words and ways of God, young people use their opinions to make their own rules. Like water running downhill, each generation moves faster and faster away from the ways of God.

Changing methods to accomplish more is commendable as long as principles are not changed. To be successful, church leaders keep adjusting teachings and programs which move away from the principles established by God. By the time the seventh millennial day arrived, religion had so watered down the words of God it was believed a person only needed the last rites of a priest or nice words from a preacher at a funeral to gain entrance into Heaven. Physical death was seen as a reconciling of differences with God. Forgiveness and acceptance by God is only granted to a person who loves God. A person, who does not experience love before his body dies, cannot love after his body dies. Death does not replace love as the way to become acceptable to God.

Television became the primary teacher of children. Children could quote chapter and verse about a movie star, a singer or an athlete but knew very little about God. These people of fame, fortune and power became the inspiration of the young and old alike. Membership in a church was considered a fulfillment of the requirement for being ok with God and reserving a place in heaven. Like actors, religious people learned the script and acted out some of the parts but that didn't change who they were.

These words are not judgments because no one can judge a person's relation to God. These words are similar to the words of God in the Old Testament and the words of Christ in the New Testament. They point our things worthy of consideration. Good works don't save and bad works don't condemn. The presence or absence of love is what saves or condemns. As Christ told Nicodemus, a person must be born from above. Loving the things and ways of this world is evidence a person is not born from above. **Do not love the world or things in the world. If someone loves the world, he does not have a love for the Father. (I John 2:15).** It is the same with humans. A man or woman who loves someone who is not their spouse does not love their spouse.

America could have been a witness for God that turned the whole world toward God but the desires and agendas of self-willed people kept adjusting downward to tolerate the desires of the flesh. Like Balaam, the people of America became so focused upon what they wanted they didn't have the clarity of vision of a jackass. They could not see a messenger of God standing in their way, trying to stop them from going the ways of Satan for wealth and prestige. (Numbers 22:1-35).

The influence of the Catholic Church was strong in America. Their way of adjusting to the evils of the people instead of standing pat on the instructions of God was a license for evil for the people serving Satan. Just as Peter adjusted the instructions of Christ, Catholic leaders continued doing the same. Pope Pius IX proclaimed the immaculate conception of Mary which decreed, unlike all other humans, Mary was free of original sin. That's a direct contradiction of what Christ told Nicodemus. Any problem caused by Paul's statement, "Everyone has sinned and is continually falling short of the glory of God" was remedied by the Vatican council declaring the pope infallible when he speaks "excathedra"(official chair patterned after the seat of Moses-Matthew 23:2-3). This was a corrupt, Jewish tradition used to serve an agenda of the Catholic Church. A mother is given a higher position of reverence than her son, causing many Catholics to address their prayers to Mary. This was a successful move by Satan to get a religious leader to authorize a human to be superior to Christ, God's word. Saying it isn't so doesn't change the edict.

The most popular of the Bibles was the translation from Greek ordered by King James. Even with its many flaws it contained priceless information about God and man. The problem arose when leaders began teaching it as a perfect, iron-clad law instead of a dim light to reveal the path to God. Texts were taken out of context to support some man's opinion. Relying upon traditional meanings of words instead of the Greek words, traditions protected by the translators, were as wrong as unauthorized edicts of the Catholic Church.

Leaders, whose rise to fame and fortune included access to the meaning of mistranslated words, refused to expose the errors, not because of ignorance, but for fear of producing a controversy that would blemish their reputation. Like the Scribes, they knew what the Scriptures said but would not go against traditions. These are examples of how fiercely the human brain will protect and defend existing knowledge. Religious traditions are as valid to religious people as the words of God.

Ekklesia is a Greek word that represents a gathering of people who are called (kalew) out (ek). Its meaning is similar to eklekto which also means called out in the sense of being chosen. Neither word means church. Church is a fabricated word that obscures the meaning. Some people who are chosen may be in the church system because they don't possess sufficient understanding of, or faith in, God to follow him without a human leader. Like the Scribes and Pharisees, they mentally learn the scriptures and mentally dedicate themselves to follow their leaders but, like Nicodemus, many don't understand what it means to be born from above. Because love is the key to a relationship with God, a lack of understanding, like that of Nicodemus, can be overcome by a love for God. It's similar to children who don't understand parents but still love them. However, teachings that don't represent God are deadly to faith.

The few (remnant) in the church system who reach the stage of being a kernel are known as the "chosen". In spite of their weaknesses caused by associating with people who replace God with religion, these chosen find a path to God. With all their flaws and incorrect knowledge, they love God. When it came to knowing about God, the people who came to America were similar to the people who came out of Egypt with Moses. The Israelites had been subjected to the religions of Egypt for 400 years. They had long since forgotten YHWH (YHVH). They faced circumstances in the wilderness that could only be endured with the help of God. America's founders used the same information that made Israel great to form their system of laws and, in time, became the most free and prosperous nation the world had ever known. Like the creation of man on the sixth day of creation, America was the creation of God during the sixth millennial day.

Just as Pharaoh wanted to keep the Israelites in bondage, the British wanted to keep America in bondage. Just as there were many differences in thinking among the people who came out of Egypt, there were many differences in the thinking of people who came from different nations, cultures and beliefs. This caused tremendous birth pains which required much patience and grace for God to help them overcome. The forty years Israel spent in the wilderness taught the people, God would provide even when they didn't deserve his help.

The signing of the declaration of independence in 1776 was America's exodus from the rule of England. The forty years that followed that exodus was a time of total dependence upon God for survival. Like the people led by Moses, signing the peace treaty of the war of 1812, ended forty years of seeing God protecting his people from a much more powerful enemy. The forming of the American Bible Society (1816) compares to the crossing of Jordan for Israel to reclaim land given them by God. America, armed with the words of God, would set out to reclaim the people captured by Satan. They would help people become what God intended them to be.

Both were times of building faith by having no choice for survival but God. Sometimes it is when a person reaches the limit of his ability and has no other options, he is best able to trust God. A person of means can survive by depending upon what he has. Why should he ask God for help if he can help himself? This is why Christ mentioned the difficulty of a rich person entering the reign of God. He doesn't have to ask God about anything material.

Both Israel and America took land inhabited by others. The difference is, God gave Israel their land and others had taken possession of it. They had no choice because the inhabitants would not willingly vacate the land. America's assignment was not reclaiming land but reclaiming people. People came to America to escape conditions they didn't like. They should have shown respect for the people who owned the land. If they had, peaceful coexistence would have permitted both to learn from each other about God and both would have been better for it. Religious knowledge prevented this happening and many evil things, opposed by God, happened during these times. The mixture of good and evil knowledge is not only seen in a person's brain, it is also seen in good and evil people.

In the same way Adam and Eve were turned from God's purpose for them, Americans were turned from God's purpose for them. Instead of being messengers of God to a noble race of people, they saw taking the possessions these people the way Adam and Eve saw taking the forbidden fruit God told them not to eat. They stopped being noble messengers of God and became murderers and robbers. They revealed the warped thinking of Satan by being upset because the innocent people resisted being killed and robbed. The particles of human dust God used to make a body for America were as different as the cells of a human body. More than once cancerous cells threatened the life of America.

Like a pendulum of a clock, the people swung back and forth between good and evil. In time, the desire of the brain for knowledge and the desire of the body for things that would produce pleasure moved God into the closet of "anything goes religion". Now they could use opinions of what God meant to make adjustments to accommodate their desires and imaginations. Using agenda-oriented teachings, religion became as corrupt in America as it had been in any other time or place. People professing to be Christians killed other people they didn't like or thought inferior. Only a few (the remnant) retained the ability to recognize the voice of Christ. Truth ceased to be the arbitrator of differences and the land began to fill with "churches" selling their opinions and agendas. Like merchants selling different products, church denominations sold different interpretations of the Bible to secure buyers and grow their businesses.

They continued to use their teachings of bribery and fear to stimulate the emotions of the people to entice or scare them into joining a church. Many people who came to America to have religious freedom possessed the same degree of intolerance as the people of the countries they left. They either didn't read or didn't believe what God told Zerubbabel. **It is not by force, nor by firmness but by my breath. (Zechariah 4:6).**

God's Breath (Christ) presents truth to a person and leaves him free to choose or not choose truth. There is no promise of heaven or fear of hell involved. Love cannot become a reality by the use of bribery or coercion. To many of the people, God was a teaching or sermon. As confidence in the teachings of the church system grew, faith in God became obsolete. In the absence of faith, psychosomatic endeavors and medical science replaced what Christ taught faith could do. A loss of respect for God, produced by empty words of preachers, emboldened many to mock the Bible and people who trusted its information.

The weakness of faith and love caused the void to be filled by physicians, lawyers and psychologists because the people no longer thought God would help them. The words of Christ, **"Everything you ask in prayer, believing, you will receive;"** and the words of Paul, **"The payment for sin is death,"** were only subjects of sermons. They were not realistic to many church people. Permitting the knowledge of the brain to outrank the words of God killed the ability to solve problems by listening to Christ, God's Breath of Truth. That part of man which enables him to trust God is dead or so weak, it won't respond to God. Christ told a man with an ill child, all things were possible to the person believing. Like so many modern, desperate parents who recognize their lack of faith, the man cried and said, "Lord, I believe! Help my lack of belief!" The man had confidence because of what he had seen and heard but he didn't have faith.

The fruit of the tree of knowledge of good and evil was/is a deadly poison. People pray to God, not with faith to heal but for him to help the physician. If all goes well they give God credit for what the physician does for them. Christ told the people, "Your faith healed you." If a person doesn't have faith, he needs to admit it and seek the help of a physician but, don't give God and faith credit for what a physician does. A physician does not use faith, he uses knowledge, skill, drugs and, if he is listening, a word of guidance from Christ. Faith does not need assistance. The first step in overcoming a lack of faith is confessing there is no faith.

When Israel entered Canaan they were told to kill everyone. No such instructions were given to the people who came to America. There was plenty of room for the inhabitants of the land and newcomers. If the newcomers had been Godly people they would have seen the inhabitants as objects of God's love. In time, both would have learned important information from each other. They supposedly represented Christ but, because the church system operated like the synagogue system, anyone expressing their faith in God differently from them was a pagan or infidel. Law, not love, was the rule.

Instead of expressing the love of Christ to the natives, the newcomers, using force supported by laws, destroyed a people more honorable than they. Evil leaders, who were members of the church system which claimed to represent God, concocted laws that made it legal to kill the original owners of the lands of America, take their land and incarcerate the women, children and old people. Men who weren't killed were incarcerated on reservations with the others. Other evil people in the church system, who were too cowardly or too far away from God to hear his voice, said it was okay because it was legal. The rule of law replaced the words of God.

Evil leaders, who were members of a church system which claimed to represent God, concocted laws that made it legal to enslave and sell black people and make them live like the mules that pulled the plows. Other evil people in the church system, who were too cowardly or too far away from God to hear his voice, said it was okay because it was legal. Hitler was considered evil, by these same people, for killing millions of people and seizing their possessions yet, he had the same legal right as the hypocritical, "God-fearing" people of America had when they terrorized the Indian and Negro. Rationalizing with legalese, the church-going people of America were convinced what they were doing was approved by God. A lie is the primary defense of an evil person.

The church system prospered and built huge, impressive idols which they called "Houses of God". These represented their imaginary god of the past and future. Their teachings and sermons indicated they didn't know the God of the present. Preachers labored diligently to prepare sermons that would please and entertain the audience. The most entertaining preacher drew the largest crowd and became pastor, imam or rabbi of the largest congregation. Most of the prosperous people attended the largest and most influential church, synagogue or mosque. There was so much darnel in the groups, there appeared to be little difference in the way these religious people lived and the way people who openly rejected the ways of God, lived. The most revealing evidence of Godlessness was the children and young people who expressed great admiration for famous people who lived lives contrary to the ways of God.

A few young people who were outspoken for God were told they couldn't talk out loud to or about God while they were in school or at a school outing. The sixth millennial day saw some evidence of love in many of the people of America even though they were shackled by the creeds of their church and laws of their government. As seen in the conduct of Peter, the pyramid system puts man in charge, lets the leader and/or the group make the rules, criticizes those who don't adhere to the rules and, like Peter, the Jewish priests, imams, and preachers actually believe they represent God.

God is Truth. Christ said knowing truth, which is "knowing God", will make a person free. Christ said he, not a man, would be so close to a person he would actually be in him. As Truth, he speaks to and guides each person who will do what he says. Peter's church system tells where Christ <u>was</u> and what he <u>did</u> but fails to tell the people where Christ <u>is</u>, what he <u>is</u> doing and how he is doing what he does. Peter's church system continues to distort God and his purpose the way he did when he founded it. It is a religious school where the same thing is taught over and over until callouses form on the heart and ears of the listeners. Christ said this is why the Jews couldn't hear the voice of God. (Matthew 13:15).

SUMMARY

Why did God create man and his universe? Since Jews, Christians and Muslims all accept what God told Moses as being authentic, that information, the information provided by Christ and what a person knows about himself will be used to answer the question. God told Moses he created another god exactly like himself. That means, to understand God, a person has to understand self. From the time males and females reach puberty, the changes in the chemistry of their bodies cause them to be physically attracted to the opposite sex. As they mature, another desire, which is nonphysical, which they don't understand, causes them to begin a search for a particular person that will satisfy this desire. The desires are different. One desire comes from the brain and body and the other desire comes from the god residing in the body.

The first desire is physical and the second desire is caused by the need for someone with whom they can share mutual love. This is when Satan gets involved to cause them to think liking someone is the same as loving someone. People like it when the physical desire is satisfied but because this is only physical, the god in the body is not satisfied. Many things can produce a liking but only love can satisfy the god in the body. This desire is not produced by sight, sound, feelings or circumstances. A love for family, friends and things will not fulfill this desire. If and when the match is found that will satisfy the craving, the union will be unbreakable. This is the mutual love of a man and woman. The human brain cannot understand or explain. It is superior to all other forms of love. It is the only thing that will produce contentment.

Some cultures choose mates for their children. This ignores the need for love which only comes with freedom of choice. Love is only possible for a god living in a human body and a match for a god in a human body can only be determined by that god. This is the same thing that occurs between a human and God. This is beyond the capacity of the brain to control or understand. This love cannot be produced, controlled or destroyed because it is a part of the substance of God who is defined as "love". Love is not produced by desire, bribery or coercion. Wanting what God has to offer or, being afraid not to accept God, will not produce love for God any more than those traits will produce love for another person.

Heaven was filled with magnificent, talented beings. Isaiah describes Lucifer as being one of the most beautiful and talented in all of Heaven. God loved Lucifer but Lucifer didn't love God. Lucifer wanted to be like God and have what he had. Many human marriages are motivated by the same desire. This desire blinded Lucifer to the love God had for him. He didn't realize God's love had already made him a part of everything he had and was. There are several forms of love. Parents love children; children love parents and friends love friends but these are not the same as love between a man and a woman whose love for each other makes them one, inseparable being. Unable to find this love in Heaven, God designed a plan to find love that would give him contentment.

The extravagance of God in preparing an entire universe as a gift for the object of his love reveals the source of the extravagance of a man trying to impress a woman or a woman looking her best to impress a man who is the object of this love. Making a god equal to him was the first thing God did. Next, this god must be put in a position where he had to choose between God and another suitor. God created a physical body for man, controlled by a brain of indefinable ability. This body had many desires which would be denied or satisfied by its brain. The god, living in this body, must make decisions to follow the instructions of God or permit his physical brain to yield to destructive desires of its body. A man and woman have strong desires for anyone of the opposite sex. They must choose to be faithful to their mate or satisfy their desires with other partners. Their decision determines if they will be united as one with a mate. This same choice is required of a god in a human body. He must choose between God and the desires of his body. Just as love produces faith, love also produces faithfulness.

As with humans, a choice must be made before a marriage can be consummated. To provide the human brain with a choice, God planted two trees with instructions to not eat of the tree of knowledge. Knowledge is to the brain what a beautiful woman is to a man. Because the brain depends upon knowledge to satisfy its needs, the tree of knowledge was extremely attractive. The god in the physical body of Adam and Eve must now decide to honor the instructions of God or pacify the desires of its brain and body. The desires of the body and emotional reasoning of the brain present a worthy opponent to the instructions of God. Without love, being faithful to God or a physical mate is an extremely difficult thing to do. Like humans, God does not want an unfaithful or self-centered mate.

The two trees God planted represented an existence based upon life and an existence based upon knowledge. One represented God, who is the source of life for the god living in the body, and the other represented knowledge which is the source of life for the physical brain. Not comprehending God, the brain did not realize the knowledge provided by God would be far more satisfying than the knowledge it would collect from other sources. The choice would determine if the brain or the god in the body ruled the total man. If Adam should choose the tree of knowledge he would be separated from the tree of life, die and his brain would be in control.

In this case, death is not ceasing to exist, it is separation from life. When a human dies physically, his body does not cease to exist; it is separated from life that permits it to function. Adam did not cease to exist; he was separated from life that enabled him to function as a god. He became a prisoner; existing in a physical body controlled by a brain whose ability was limited to its choices between knowledge that produced good and knowledge that produced evil. This dependence upon knowledge instead of God would guide Adam into many problems and eventually death.

Another god joined the challenge as an adversary. He would influence the brain to make decisions that would harm man.

Lucifer, whose attraction to God was motivated by what God had, was jealous because God created another god who was everything God was. Lucifer's name became Satan which means "adversary". He became the adversary of both, God and Adam. Because a part of the mental weakness of a woman is pleasing speech and intrigue, Satan appeared in the physical form of a serpent which could impress her with its smooth talk and stimulating movements. The stimulation produced by these movements is the reason men and women want to dance. He appealed to the desires of Eve's body and the imaginations of her brain. She bought what he was selling.

Because a man's weakness is a woman, especially the most beautiful woman who ever lived, Satan used her to sell his lie to Adam. God arrived and told Adam he would have to live with the choice he made. For the remainder of his life he would not have access to information provided by life; he would have to rely upon the choices his brain would make between knowledge that produced good and knowledge that produced evil. It wasn't long before he saw what that would do for him. His first two sons had different religious ideas. Circumstantial evidence suggests Cain became angry because his younger brother killed an animal as a way of making an offering to God. There is no scriptural evidence to justify what Abel did but, there is no justification for Cain killing Abel.

There is no record of God telling Abel to sacrifice an animal. 2,000 years later Jacob made a sacrifice using an animal. No reason is given why he did that but it became a practice of his descendants and other inhabitants of the earth. Sacrificing a living thing was common among people who moved away from the ways of God. The reason given to Pharaoh for letting the people leave Egypt was to sacrifice to God. They could not perform the sacrifices in Egypt because the Egyptians considered animals, which would be sacrificed, sacred.

Killing is not an act of love. An offering to a god of love is not made by killing a living creature. Through the centuries God has worked with man on his level of understanding, the way parents work with children on their level of understanding. What was called a sacrifice, using an animal or fowl as a victim, was really a murder of an innocent animal or fowl. The callousness developed by the murder of animals and fowls for sacrifices made it easy to murder Christ. The words of Micah, the prophet of God, represent the thinking of God more closely than the sacrifice of Abel or Jacob.

How will I come before the Lord and bow before the high God? Will I come before him with burnt offerings and one year old calves? Will the Lord be pleased with thousands of rams or ten thousand rivers of oil? Should I give my firstborn for my transgressions, the fruit of my body for the sin of my soul? He has shown you, o man what is good. What does the lord require of you? You are to do justly, love mercy and walk humbly with your God. (Micah 6:6-8-KJV). If killing was a way to please to God, why is it not done today? Killing, as a way of pleasing some idea of God, is done by the most primitive people. The people who left Egypt with Moses were more primitive than the Egyptians.

Adam lived 960 years as a prisoner in his body. Each generation of his descendants made more and more choices using knowledge that produced evil results. About 600 years after Adam died the people of the earth were 100% evil except for one man. God met with this man and told him the people of the earth were going to be destroyed. He told him to build a huge boat. A huge boat where there was no water, made no sense to Noah's brain but he did what Adam didn't do; he trusted God and began building the boat.

Twenty years later his wife bore triplet sons. When these sons reached the age when they wanted wives, the only available women were those whose thoughts were constantly evil. They each selected one of these women. This was a problem waiting to happen. It took Noah another 100 years, after the birth of his sons, to complete the boat. When he completed the other instructions God gave him, he went inside this boat sitting upon dry ground and closed the door. Then nature, not God, unleased its destructive force upon all air breathing surface creatures. One hundred and twenty years of warning the people did not change them. Pacifying the desires of their bodies had produced a reprobate mind, void of understanding.

When God presented his gift of the world to Adam, he told him it was under his authority. Adam only had to think a thought and anything in his world would immediately respond. The force that enabled him to do this was faith. Faith is a single thought without conflict. With a collection of conflicting information, a person has to get conflicting thoughts to become a single thought before he can have faith. Because of the difficulty of doing this, he has little if any ability to control anything beyond the power of what his brain can produce.

His love for evil is comparable to an alcoholic's love for alcohol. He acts like someone inebriated who has lost control of common sense. Without faith, man does not have the ability to control earth, a gigantic vehicle traveling through space. Suppose a person is driving his car while he is drunk. He loses control, it crashes and he is killed. He alone is responsible for his death. He can't blame the manufacturer who built the car or the person who gave him the car. Man can't blame God for the actions of nature if he has become inebriated with the mind-altering things of this world. Nature responds to man the way man responds to God. Often, there is collateral damage caused by a drunk and nature.

All authority belongs to God but he delegated authority to man. This is why Christ said he had all authority. Like God's authority, man's authority was to be exercised by the power of faith. When God relinquished his authority, man, whose evil destroyed his faith, no longer had control of his world. Like a pet tiger turning on its master, nature turned on man. God's words, "I will destroy man" was done by withdrawing his overriding authority over nature. He left man to deal with nature and nature destroyed man. The cause was not God but man's sin which destroyed his faith. The term "wrath of God" is often misunderstood. God's wrath is not an action by God; it is the absence of God's protection. It is the same as a parent, not protecting a self-willed child, rebelliously doing things that cause him harm.

The new population consisted of eight people. One of the sons of Noah was referred to as Nephilim because, except for his family, he was the only male who lived before and after the flood. (Genesis

6:4). The Nephilim were referred to as "sons of God". Because the wives were women who were among the evil people of the pre-flood world, they were referred to as "daughters of men". The translation "men of renown" is misleading. The Hebrew word is shem; the name of a son of Noah. The Nephilim were the male descendants of Shem who was the father of the Semites who came to be known as "Israel" whose people were known as sons of God. Intermarriage with women, who were from other kinds of people, was a major cause of the downfall of Israel. Solomon is an example of that. The theory nonphysical male creatures mated with physical women, is not supported by the text.

Man can collect and use knowledge that produces things that are good or collect and use knowledge that produces evil. Each person must make this choice. The choice made is seen in each generation being more evil than the one before. After 300 years of this downward trend, the population was again filled with evil people, ignorant of God. God found one man, named Abram (Abraham) who had enough faith to help him continue his plan. Abram's faith in God was defeated by time. He didn't have patience to wait for the son God promised him. He sired a son by a woman who wasn't his wife. Just as Adam was persuaded by Eve to doubt God, Abram was persuaded by Sarah to doubt God. The firstborn son was denied the customary inheritance of the firstborn. This led to the descendants of Ishmael becoming enemies of the descendants of Isaac.

Isaac's son Jacob was a deceiver and, Jacob's sons were jealous and self-serving. Their lack of faith to trust God led them to Egypt where their descendants became slaves of the Egyptians. They lived in Egypt 400 years before God selected a man he could use, to deliver them. Moses, the son of a slave, spent forty years as an adopted son of Pharaoh's daughter. He spent another forty years as an escaped criminal who had murdered an Egyptian. His last forty years was spent as an extension of God. God talked with him as one man talking to another. This was the way God talked to Adam.

God told Moses what he had done and how mankind had responded to him from the beginning of time to the time when he talked with him. God gave him instructions which consisted of knowledge which would produce good things for the people and their descendants. Sometimes they used this knowledge and sometimes they adjusted it to accommodate their desires and circumstances. The instructions were given to train the brain to make decisions that would produce good results but the instructions were constantly adjusted by the people.

The next 200+ years were spent reclaiming most of the land God gave Abram. God used men called prophets to help the people know and remember the instructions God gave them to produce good results. Often these instructions would be in conflict with the desires of the people. There was a constant struggle between good and evil. Finally they told God's prophet they wanted a king to tell them how to live and be responsible for their well-being. They replaced God with a large man named Saul. The size of his intelligence did not match the size of his body so, he failed as a leader.

He was replaced with David, a man of courage and confidence in God. His dedication was defeated by his desire for another man's wife. This caused him to misuse the position God gave him and commit adultery and murder. His illegitimate son, Solomon, proved his reputation of being wise was greatly exaggerated. He was the worst sex pervert known to man. His extravagance required taxes that placed heavy burdens upon the people. It never fails; a self-centered person will always cause hardships for others. The heavy burdens on the people, begun by Solomon, were continued by his calloused son Rehoboam, who caused ten of the twelve tribes to revolt and separate from the nation of Israel. They lost their identity by intermarrying with the Samaritans. (The sons of God married daughters of men.)

The tribes of Judah and Benjamin continued as representatives of God. Little-by-little the instructions God gave Moses were adjusted to satisfy desires and circumstances. When Christ arrived with the truth and authority of God, the leaders didn't like what he said. They killed him. In spite of their ignorance, God accomplished his purpose. The battle Christ fought against his brain in Gethsemane was the beginning of THE GREAT DAY OF ALMIGHTY GOD called Harmageddon (Mountain Megiddo). Contrary to tradition, it was not the cross where the battle was won, it was in Gethsemane. Adam lost his battle when he permitted his brain to control him and disobey what God told him. Christ won his battle by refusing to let his brain control him and kill his body in Gethsemane. He insisted upon fulfilling the will of God. The world again had a sire that could produce children with life.

Man's battle is between him (a god) and his brain. It was in gethsemane that Christ won the battle over his brain. Man's brain is where a person's battles are fought. Christ did not qualify as a sacrifice for two reasons. First, the Passover Lamb had to be without spot or blemish. After his battle in Gethsemane and the torture he endured at the hands of his captors, he had many spots and blemishes. Second, if his dying on a cross produced redemption, why would others, dying on a cross, not produce redemption?

Christ came into the world to reverse what Adam did, by maintaining control over his brain throughout his life. Neither his brain nor the cross could kill his body. His body died when he gave it permission to die. When the Father was walking away from him he asked, **For what purpose are you leaving me behind?** Forsake is not correct. Egkatelipes means, to leave behind. Forsake means to have nothing more to do with a person or thing. God was only stepping aside because what needed to be done must be done by Christ, alone. This happens to everyone walking with God. There are times when he leaves a person to accomplish something without his help. This is necessary for someone aspiring to be like a parent.

The one who had raised the dead and healed all manner of physical malady was now faced with his own physical death. The brain will fight to keep the body from dying until circumstances overcome its ability. No circumstances could overcome the ability of Christ. If Christ had listened to his brain, he would have refused to die. It was his decision to again exercise authority over his brain and vacate his body. He, not his brain, would make the decision. He was in complete control. His words, "It is finished", were his exit from his body by his authority. He had completed his mission to provide mankind with another choice for life. He would now go to people who died before him to tell them they had a second chance to make a choice for life or death.

In the days of the voice of the seventh messenger, when he is about to blow his trumpet, the mystery of God, as it was proclaimed by his servants the prophets, will be finished (10:7). The sixth poured out his bowl upon the great river Euphrates and its waters were dried to prepare the way for the kings of the rising sun. I saw from the mouth of the great serpent, from the mouth of the small wild animal and from the mouth of the false prophet, three unclean breaths with the likeness of frogs. These are demonic breaths producing signs. They are going to the rulers of the whole earth to gather them together for the war of <u>The Great Day of Almighty God</u>. Be aware; my coming is like that of a thief. Blessed is the person who is on guard and keeps his clothes so he won't be walking around naked with others looking at his shame. He gathered them in a place the Hebrews call Harmageddon. The seventh poured out his bowl upon the air and a loud voice out of the temple from the throne repeatedly said, "It is finished." (Revelation 16:12-17) Compare John 19:30.

This was not <u>a</u> great day of Almighty God it was <u>the</u> great day of Almighty God. This was the single greatest day of the accomplishments of God. He entered a human body operated by its brain. When that brain experienced overwhelming sadness caused by the rejection of the people he loved, great pressure was in his heart. According to Luke, the pressure caused a coronary thrombosis to such an extreme, blood seeped through the pores of his skin and fell upon the ground. Even modern medical ability couldn't overcome a condition that severe. Adam permitted his brain to kill him; Christ did not. Because this is different from traditional teachings, the reader will have to decide which is the most scripturally accurate. Reading the words of Micah a few pages back may help the reader decide concerning the idea of sacrifices. Christ was not a sacrifice; he was a conqueror.

It would seem a man who spent about 3 ½ years listening to Christ and seeing the miraculous things he did would be completely convinced anything Christ said should be followed without question or adjustment. Not so with Peter. Just before Christ ascended he instructed the people present how they should carry out his plan to let people know about him. The word "go" is not an imperative (command), it is a participle. The correct translation is "as you are going". As people go about their normal routine, they talk with each other about different things. Christ told them to include in their conversations, the information they learned from him. This natural way of spreading a message is successfully used by people who represent the ways of Satan.

Instead of trusting the words of Christ, Peter trusted the reasoning of his brain. He had spent his life in a synagogue system where people were not free to make their own decisions. They were controlled by rules, regulations and teachings, with leaders who would enforce them.

He persuaded a number of believers, this was the way to do what Christ had instructed. It wasn't long after he organized this group that a man and his wife broke one of his rules. Peter murdered them. Then to justify his satanic act he said God did it. This man who often tried to correct Christ, who said he was willing to die for Christ and then denied him, has now killed two people and blamed God for it. This is the founder and leader of the Church System.

Another man named Saul was also programmed by the synagogue system. He was putting Christians in prison and killing them. Christ spoke to him with sound because his brain was blocking out communication from within. When God speaks with sound, the sound does not travel through the ear; it is above the body and is not only heard but also seen. With Paul's situation, others present heard the sound of the voice but didn't understand any words or see anyone. Saul learned Christ was in the people he was persecuting. He was a well-educated man taught by Gamaliel, a leading authority regarding information about God. His confidence in what he learned made the idea of a formally uneducated carpenter being the Messiah, bazaar.

Now, after having that error in judgment corrected, he saw the apostles as being ignorant men when it came to a question about God. Instead of finding them to learn what Christ taught them, he went into the Northern area of Saudi Arabia to rethink his theology. Later he met with Peter and James but stated they had nothing to tell him he didn't already know. His learning had made him arrogant. Several of his teachings are in conflict with Christ and a major teaching contradicts Christ. Like Peter, he thought converts should be gathered into a group like a synagogue system. The conduct of Peter and Paul indicates God will use people in spite of their ignorance and flaws. If he required perfect people, he would have no one qualified to help him.

The arrogant attitude of Paul is seen in modern preachers who find it difficult to believe Christ might tell an uneducated or unaccomplished person a truth they don't know.

With two leaders like Peter and Paul, it is not surprising in less than sixty years after the ascension of Christ the church system was corrupt. About 90 A. D. Christ took John, now in his seventies, above time, to show him the contrast between the people of the world and Heaven. Satan was using religion, government and commerce to persuade or force people to do what he wanted. Seven represents completion or all of something. The seven church systems he showed John represented all church systems. All but one had problems worthy of a reprimand. This shows some people used knowledge from the tree of knowledge that produced good. This was the group referred to as "the remnant". When looking at the total church system, most of the activity was evil.

When Christ showed John the church system, one group made him sick at his stomach. He felt like vomiting them out of his mouth. He showed John four horses and riders which represented the nature of government. Horses represent great physical power. The white horse and rider represented conquest. Governments use laws and force to conquer its own people and others. The red horse and rider represented anger. Laws permit a few in government to dominate citizens which causes a natural reaction of anger.

The third horse was black which represents poverty. When government rules impede individual effort, it leaves people without the means and ability to support themselves. In finding ways to supply their needs, government takes the initiative away from citizens and forces them to depend upon it. People become like children or slaves waiting for a hand-out. When working people are made inactive by an incompetent government, poverty prevails. The fourth horse is black and its rider's name is death. Governments are constantly marshalling their people for war where they are killing and being killed.

Christ showed John the power of commerce. The driving force of commerce is greed. The advice of Christ to treat others as you want to be treated is not a popular concept in commerce. When a person is content, Christ will show him how to make what he has be enough. This is what he told a soldier. Satan uses greed, a product of the human brain, to persuade people to strive to satisfy their desires for material things. Greed is like a growing cancer; it is never satisfied.

A young man who possessed great wealth asked Christ what he had to do to be saved. Christ began his answer by telling him to do things moral, religious people do. The young man told Christ he had always done these things. Christ then told him he needed to do one more thing; he needed to sell his possessions, give the money to the poor and follow him. The rich young man refused to do that. Then Christ explained the difficulty a rich person has, making God more important than his wealth.

Wealth can be a tool to help others or a weapon to control others and self. The moment a person can't let go of his possessions is the moment his possessions take control of him. This is illustrated in the story of Brer Rabbit and the tar baby. Christ asked a question, "What is the benefit if a person acquires the whole world and in doing that, loses his life." The beautiful things of love and life are too valuable to trade for things that become useless for a person when his body dies.

During the first 270 years after Christ ascended, the church system grew in numbers and strength. There was knowledge that produced good results but, most of the knowledge gave way to desires and imaginations of the body and brain and produced evil results. There were many ideas and writings about God and Christ that caused much confusion. About 297 A. D. the church system joined with the Roman Government to decide which writings were the most authentic and accurate. The result was the 66 writings that make up what became known as the Bible. This would have been a great improvement if it had been made available to the common man.

Church leaders didn't think the common man had sufficient intelligence to understand the writings so, a church leader told the people the meaning of the statements in the Bible. From this came teachings that were as rigid as the laws of Judaism. Two teachings were prominent which gave the church system control over the people. The first was bribery. People were told if they accepted the teachings of the priests; became a member of the church and, were baptized, God would approve them for Heaven. At times, dipping pits, used to dip livestock, were filled with water and people walked through the water. Submerging themselves while walking through the water was accepted as being "baptized" which was a part of the requirement for being saved.

The other teaching was a threat for people not joining the church or causing problems for the church. Two words used by Christ, which explained a condition associated with a person's life, were used to threaten people with Hell. Hell is a made-up word which was a false translation of the two words used by Christ (gehenna and haides). This made people afraid not to be a part of the church system. People came to believe this so strongly the prime leader, who came to be called "pope", exercised power over everyone including kings. The church convinced people the pope had the power to excommunicate them and send them straight to this imaginary hell. There always seemed to be a few people who listened to God speaking truth directly to them, who didn't buy the lies taught by the church system.

Each generation produced more corruption in the church system. In 570 A. D. a baby was born who was named Muhammad.

When he was six, his mother died and left him an orphan. When he was 25, he married a rich widow. When he was 40, God began speaking to him and giving him instructions that would help him know the power of love. The writings became known as the "Quran". Like Peter, God offered him an opportunity to help him help people but, just as Peter took the good knowledge Christ gave him and used it for his own purposes, Muhammad took the good knowledge God gave him and used it to advance his agenda. Like peter, he ignored what God told him, collected the people into organizations and made himself their leader. Ten years later he began robbing caravans and killing people who opposed him.

The church system ignored the evil which Peter did and Islam ignored the evil which Muhammad did and made them heroes for God. This made doing evil, like them, acceptable conduct for their followers. Forcing people to accept his opinion of God is not what Christ did. Each person must choose to follow people like Peter and Muhammad or follow Christ. These two men did not deny self and follow Christ. The people who will deny self and follow Christ are few and are called "a remnant". Good intentions and good deeds are not what make a person acceptable to God.

Jews, Christians and Muslims are the three groups of people who trace a common lineage back to Abraham. Many of them have the same mental deficiency as Cain. Their intolerance of religious differences of others voids any possibility of God's love controlling them. They become people possessed of demons. There were/are many deaths caused by the fleshy zeal of all three. Like the Jews, Muslims and Christians resorted to the Old Testament instructions for physical conquest for land and ignored what Christ taught about love and truth. The physical conquests, with all their horror, were parallels to the conquest of self. Evil desires and imaginations have to be killed or driven out before a person can have peace. It is not the ways of Jews, Peter and Muhammad but the ways of Christ that produce inner peace and prosperity. True prosperity is not material things but things like love, joy, peace, faith, etc.

Each generation moved farther away from Christ into the errors of Judaism, Christianity and Islam. Ignorance was king. There were centuries called "the dark ages" when Christ, the light of the world, was close to an eclipse. The King James Bible was a translation made by men who were known as Greek and Hebrew scholars. In addition to being a scholar, a person must be honest if he intends doing work for God. If they were honest, why did they incorrectly translate some words and transliterate others. The answer to that question is; the traditions inherited from the Catholic Church had to be protected.

Greek words like ayyelos, baptidzo, mamonas and hupokrites were transliterated leaving the reader without understanding of their meaning. The Hebrew letter yod (y) and the Greek letter iota (i) were changed to J. This was done to preserve the traditional names Jesus and Jehovah. These two errors are exposed by the Hebrew word YHWH (YHVH-mistranslated Jehovah) and by the fish symbol seen on vehicles and other places. The name in the symbol is I X Θ Y Σ (Ichthus). The first letter is not J; the first letter is I. When transferring a name from one language to another the name is transliterated; using letters equivalent to the original language. Gabriel told Mary to call her baby, Iesous. Jesus is a nickname. When used for a long time, a nickname becomes a common way of addressing a person. God, like people, becomes accustomed to answering to a nickname.

The Greek word aion means life as in a lifespan. The word aionios means without beginning or end as in forever or eternity. Christ did not tell his people he would be with them to the end of the world. They wouldn't be in the world after their body died; they would be in Heaven. He said he would be with them to the end of their life span. (Matthew 28:20). The word kosmos (world) is not in the text. Another error is in Revelation 1:1. The tense of the Greek word ginesthai can be aorist (past tense) or present tense. This word identifies the information in Revelation as being about past events or present conditions. Nothing in Revelation refers to the future. The White Throne Court is in session, now. The New Jerusalem, descending from Heaven to earth, exists now. It is not brick and mortar; it is saved people. Unless a distinction is made between the physical and nonphysical, the agenda of God will not be understood.

Anothen is a Greek word that was translated incorrectly in John 3:3 but correctly in John 3:31; 6:13; 8:23; 19:11. The translation "born again" in 3:3 leaves a reader without understanding of what Christ was telling Nicodemus. The correct translation "born from above" explains how life can move from one level of existence to a higher level of existence because of the magnetic attraction of the higher form of life. Life in the soil can become life in a kernel of corn which can become life in an animal which can become life in a human.

The Greek words gehenna and haides were the ones used by the church system to scare people into joining the church. Gehenna (ge'enna) was a valley South and East of Jerusalem which came to be a dump for garbage and dead carcasses. By reading the eleven statements of Christ where he used this word, it is evident he is speaking of decisions a person makes in life that can cause that person to have a life filled with things like that which exists in a landfill. Hades means "inability to see". Just as darkness causes physical blindness, ignorance causes mental blindness. The six times Christ used the word hades, he is referring to ignorance like that of the rich man whose concern was his pain and not the cause of his pain. A person addicted to opinions, habits, drugs and other things wants relief from the pain but is ignorant of a will and way to stop the cause of the pain. Incorrect knowledge is evil knowledge and produces evil results.

Near the end of the sixth day, America elected her fortieth president. Forty is an important number in Jewish gramatria. It took forty days of rain to prepare the world for a new generation of people. With Moses there were three periods of forty in his life. The first forty ended after he completed his life as a ruler in Egypt. The second forty ended after he completed his life as a common man among common people. The third forty ended after he prepared Israel to take the land God gave them. Israel spent forty years in the wilderness learning how to trust God. Moses spent forty days in the mountain without eating or drinking before God gave him the ten instructions for Godly living. Christ spent forty days without food and drink preparing for his assignment. He spent forty days on earth after his resurrection preparing his followers for their assignment. Forty represents the time required for something to complete incubation and begin a new phase.

America's election of President Reagan, her fortieth president, began a severe downward trend for America. His vice president had a questionable tract record which continued as decisions were made to do things illegal and harmful to people. A little known governor of a small state was enlisted to aid in this illegal, undercover activity. After the vice president's four year term, the governor was rewarded by being supported by the "establishment" to become the 42nd president. He began dismantling the job market, causing many people to look to the government for their livelihood. He was followed by a man of wealth and influence whose value of a dollar was much different from that of a working man.

At the end of his term he used his authority to direct funds, needed for businesses which produced jobs, to his wealthy friends. This increased the dependence of the people upon government which had to depend upon the people for the money needed to provide for the people. The idiocy was like a dog chasing his tail. His decision produced a merry-go-round ready to collapse. These are prime examples of self-centered leadership. The government printed money and continued on the road to insolvency. This president was followed by a man of little experience who was a puppet of the powerful people who select world leaders. He said he was a Christian but he made many statements and decisions which attacked the beliefs of Christians and aided the evil faction of Islam whose goal was to destroy America.

By the end of his term, all three branches of the government had become a "me first" group of people. The press added to the decline by printing and saying things that made them producers and manipulators of news instead of reporters of news. Lies and baseless accusations were the weapons of choice. They appeared to assume the people were too ignorant to know what they were doing. America was no longer ruled by a government of the people, for the people and by the people. America was ruled by a government of the government, for the government and by the government. Finally, soon after the beginning of the seventh millennial day, enough of the people revolted to elect a man who gave them hope of better times.

ORIGINAL DAY SEVEN: PAUSE, PROPOSE AND CLEAN

1. God ended his work on the seventh day:
2. God stopped, interrupted or paused on the seventh day (rested).
3. God kneeled on the seventh day (blessed).
4. God cleaned on the seventh day (sanctified).

The number seven represents completion. Not recognizing one statement produced a tradition that is not supported by the text in Genesis 2:2-3. Without actually saying the words, tradition teaches God completed his work on the sixth day and did nothing on the seventh day. It is clearly stated; God completed his work on the seventh day. If a person completes something he is doing on a certain day, that day is mentioned, not the day after or day before. If God had completed his work on the sixth day, that would be the day stated in the text. God was still active on the seventh day.

Translations were made to accommodate the tradition. A more definitive word for rest is pause. The word paused could mean rest but only for a short period of time. The correct word for bless is kneel. This is an act of adoration. A man who proposes to the woman he loves, kneels before her as an act of adoration. God kneeled in adoration of the god he created for his mate and proposed. The day a man and woman agree to marry is remembered as a special day. The seventh day was a special day for God for the same reason. It was the day he took the new god on a tour of what he had done and proposed.

Sanctified means, "to clean". God didn't clean the seventh day he cleaned on the seventh day. Paul's opinion about people who make one day more important than another was: **Indeed, this one is**

choosing a day from a day (making one day more important than another) **but that one is choosing all days. Let each be confident in his mind. (Romans 14:5).** The Hebrew word "shabath" means to rest in the sense of pausing from previous activity. The Hebrew word "shaba" means seven, complete or full. The previous activity was creating things. Whatever was left of the creating phase was completed on the seventh day. Physical bodies for man and the creatures were formed after the first seven days.

When a phase of a construction project appears to be complete, there is a pause in the work and an inspection is begun to make certain the work matches the plan. Inspecting and adjusting, which includes cleaning the site, was done on the seventh day. God completed the creating part of his work on the sixth day when he created man. Then, on the seventh day, he and man began inspecting what he had done. Like a man showing off for his intended, God was showing man the wonderful place he prepared as a place for the two of them to live.

During the first four days he created non-life forms to accommodate the needs of life forms he would create. The number four came to represent the world. On day five he created life for nonhuman creatures. On day six he created life in the form of another god like him. None of the life forms had physical bodies. Now, the project has reached the seventh day when this phase of God's work will be completed. Beginning on day seven, God and man began working together to make what God did, evolve into the completion of God's total agenda.

At the end of the seventh original day God began to dwell with all he had created and made. The eighth day began a new phase of his plan. In this phase he made physical bodies for man and other creatures and planted a garden where they would live. The created god (Adam) was the first to receive a body and after that all the other physical forms were made. (Genesis 2:5; 19). Birds and animals were made to be companions for comfort, aid and entertainment for the male/female god named Adam who lived in one physical human body. These would satisfy the emotional needs of their physical brain but nothing God made could fulfill their need for contentment. (Genesis 2:20). Neither they nor God would be content until Adam, a duplicate of God, chose God as the fulfillment of his need for love.

This gives insight into the reason God made man. Heaven was populated with perfect beings that could comfort God, help him with whatever he wanted to do and even entertain him but, none could satisfy God's basic need for love. Love needs contentment and it takes a special person or god to produce contentment. Man is like God. All the citizens of heaven were to God what friends and families are to humans. They provided a mutual form of love that produced satisfaction but could not produce contentment. There is only one love of humans that produces contentment and that is the mutual love of a man and woman. God needed someone his equal who would love him above all others and everything in existence. In the same way, there is no love on earth that can give a human contentment except a spouse whose shares mutual love. Like the number seven, contentment is completion or perfection.

Contentment is not produced by people and things but by love for an equal that returns that love. There are other loves that can be shared with family, friends and pets that can give a degree of satisfaction but these will not produce contentment. Just as nothing God made on earth could fulfill this need for man, nothing he made in heaven could fulfill his need. Human contentment comes when one man and one woman are made one by love. Godly contentment comes when God and people who form a nonphysical body are made one by love. Individuals who return God's love are made one with God. Just as particles of dust became the body of Adam and particles of Mary's body became the physical body of Christ, Each saved person will be a nonphysical particle of the body of God.

God said, **"It is not good that man should be alone. I will make from him, a help meet for him."** The Hebrew word for Adam and man is the same. In Genesis 2:23, 24 the statements should read, "taken from or separated from the male". **The Lord formed every beast of the field and every fowl of the air from the ground and brought them to Adam to see what he would call them. The name of every living creature was what Adam**

called them. Adam gave names to every dumb beast, to the fowls of the air and every living thing of the fields but there was not found a succorer for him. The Lord God caused a deep sleep to fall upon Adam and while he slept he took one of his ribs and closed the depression. He made a woman with the rib which he took from man (male and female in one body) and brought her to the man. (Genesis 2:18-24).

A succorer is someone who can surround, as in an embrace. Because man is like God, God is like man; both need someone to succor them. No one can succor like the object of one's love. It is easy to see the parallel of what God did and why he made man. Just as he used a part of the first body to make a body for Eve, he used a part of himself to make a nonphysical being like himself. Just as nothing he made from the earth was an appropriate mate for man, nothing he made in Heaven was an appropriate mate for him. His instructions were, "A male (different from the word for Adam and man) should leave his father and mother (the objects of his greatest love), and cling to his wife. This is what God did when he left Heaven to cling to humanity by becoming a human. In spite of everything man has done to forfeit God's love, God continues to love man; demonstrating, love is something that cannot be destroyed.

In the phase that began after the first seven days, man must freely love God above all else for there to be contentment for both God and man. This is the basis for marriage between a man and a woman. The choice would decide if man would become a mate for God or, love what would please his brain and body. Every human born into this world is faced with the same choice. No one but God knows for certain but, assuming all followed the lead of Adam, every human, with sufficient mental ability to make a responsible choice, makes the choice that kills him. That's why God, in Christ, gave humans a second chance to make a choice.

Something Peter said had to be told by Christ during the forty days he was with the apostles after he arose and before he ascended. **Christ suffered once as a sinner; a just *person* in behalf of an unrighteous *person*, so he could lead you to God. He, indeed, was killed physically but was made alive as breath. In this**

form he also went and spoke to the breath beings kept under guard. (1 Peter 3:18-19). Peter warned the people to whom he was writing, about the people who were criticizing them because they didn't show proper hospitality. They were being criticized for refusing to participate in their pagan feasts. He said the words of these critics are actually spoken to the one who judges the living and dead. **They are speaking to the one prepared, having judged the living and dead. This is the reason he proclaimed good news to the dead so they could be judged by the breath of God as men living in bodies (1 Peter 4:5-6).**

All who died before Christ were ignorant of what he would do for them. They were kept under guard in outer darkness or in paradise. Physically, outer darkness is the area beyond the water which was separated from the water which became earth. Darkness represents an inability to see and is a metaphor for ignorance. Christ told the Jewish leaders they, and people like them, who are not dressed in the righteousness of Christ and, people who refuse to use what God gives them, would be sent to outer darkness which is a state of continued ignorance. (Matthew 8:12; 22:13; 25:30). He also said the barriers of ignorance (darkness) would not prevent God speaking to an ignorant person the way he spoke to Peter concerning the identity of Christ. Christ went to the people who had died to tell them they had a second chance to trust God and be restored to life.

The first phase of God's work of the old creation ended at the end of the seventh original day. The first phase of God's work of the new creation in Christ will end at the end of the seventh millennial day. On the seventh original day God completed the first phase of his work, paused, and kneeled in adoration of man. The instructions in Exodus 20:8-11 are instructions to not perform work that was reserved for the other six days. It does not forbid all activity. The words holy and sanctified are instructions for cleanliness which required some effort. The word rest does not mean cessation of all activity; it means to pause before continuing with what he was doing. On the seventh day God did what a bridegroom would normally do as he is showing his bride plans for the future.

In the same way physical bodies were not made until after the seven original days, the heavenly bodies of the redeemed are not made until after the seventh millennial day. Each body is made to accommodate its capacity for love, joy, peace etc. That which is seen as rewards for people who receive the gift of love and become citizens of Heaven is not status or wealth but abilities to appreciate what they are. Just as there are degrees of love in different humans in physical bodies, this is also true of God's people after they leave their body. The degree to which a person loves determines the intensity of his experience. Some people have a greater capacity than others. This corresponds to the story Christ told about the three men who received ten, five and one talent. (Matthew 25:14-30).

The end of the first seven original days began many days of good and bad activities for man and God. The end of the seven millennial days will begin a new day that has no end and no mental knowledge to cause conflict. When the last second of the seventh millennial day expires, a new, timeless day will begin.

MILLINNIAL DAY SEVEN:
6,000-7,000- (2,000-3,000 A. D.)
PAUSE, PROPOSE AND CLEAN

America entered the seventh millennial day filled with all forms of evil and some good. Religion, government and commerce ruled the people. Religion adjusted the meaning of love and truth to accommodate young people who didn't know or want God. These grow up to produce other generations worse than they. Unbelief in the words of God convinces many; scientists know more about creation than God. They appeared to be ignorant of the fact a person can't believe God without believing what God says. Government continues dominating the people with self-centered leadership. With greed-stimulating sales people, commerce entices people so far into debt, any sickness or error subjects them to bankruptcy or homelessness.

Religions, which contradict each other, minimize their differences by compromising their beliefs about God. Because everyone has a right to their opinion, God is obligated to approve everyone. Government so divides the people, anger (the red horse) is the norm for political opinions. Commerce keeps enticing people by making them think they must have the latest gadget, newest car or most impressive house to prove their equality. Satan is well pleased with the work his demons and human messengers are doing to defeat God's America the way he defeated God's first man. The seventh millennial day is like the home stretch in a tract meet. Satan's time is drawing to a close. He will use everything he has to defeat God and man.

The day Christ died was The Great Day of Almighty God. It was the day of Armageddon when Satan was exiled to earth where, instead of accusing man to God, he accuses God to man. He is a god not subject to time or a physical body but, his exile to earth means his attack on a person is limited to the ability of that person. To him, the time remaining before God deletes time is short. He has to use all his wits to defeat as many people as he can. Christ defeated him in Gethsemane but, as a sore loser, he can still vent his anger by blinding people to the reality of life and death.

His goal is to use things like suffering, wealth and anger to make God look unfaithful, unnecessary or non-existent. No matter how much he lies and belittles, he can't seem to fool 100% of the people. There is always a small percentage of the population who believes what God says. The seventh millennial day is his last chance to succeed. **Calamity to the earth and the sea (the total population of the earth) because the deceiver has, with great anger, come down to you, knowing he has a small amount of time. (Revelation 12:12b).**

The sixth millennial day ended with the world in turmoil. Most of the people of America say they believe in God but their speech and conduct has little resemblance to the words and ways of Christ. The mixture of good and evil knowledge is predominantly evil. Since millennial day seven just began, predictions about it must be based upon what happened on the seventh original day and man's tract record for the past 6,000 years. On the seventh original day God completed the first phase of his work, paused, made his proposal to man and cleaned the job site.

The seventh millennial day began with the nations of the world on the brink of war. Most of America's leaders in religion, government and commerce were striving to climb the ladder of success. In the 2016 election, a woman with little respect for truth received a majority of the votes of the people of America. This indicates more than half of the people of America are committed to Satan, the father of liars. She was defeated by a man of wealth who appears to embrace the ways of God but is not well informed about some details taught by Christ. Like David was to Israel, he may be the best God can find to help him prolong the life of America. This election clearly revealed the hostile division which existed in the nation formed and blessed by God.

Corruption in government had caused hardships for the people. Greed in commerce had produced a few who were wealthy but most struggled to survive. The desire for status and wealth caused religion to adjust the words of Christ to accommodate young and old whose ambitions were linked the material things of the world. These three forces used by Satan to control people were serving him well. America, like Adam, liked the taste of the fruit of the tree of knowledge of good and evil. Saying and doing good things became the way to salve the conscious for evil attitudes, speech and activity.

Churches had become businesses and pastors and priests were the CEOs of these businesses. These leaders found different ways to attract people to their churches. Sometimes it was by declaring a strict adherence to the traditional interpretations of the Bible and sometimes it was by adopting the style of entertainment used by Hollywood. There was very little, if any, resemblance to the simple Godliness demonstrated by Christ. They had similar characteristics to social clubs. Like the Scribes and Pharisees, their righteousness quickly turned to anger for any person who challenged them.

Just as children, taught by irresponsible mothers, are usually irresponsible; legislators, judges and presidents taught by irresponsible clergy are usually irresponsible. The great nation America; became more and more rotten from the inside. Believing mentally generated knowledge was the solution for solving its problems added to the speed of its downfall. There is too much conflict in mentally generated knowledge for it to resolve opposing views but, leaders continue to say education is the solution to problems. This would be true if the education was learning the words and ways of Christ. Many people are willingly ignorant. Their mind is made up. Don't confuse them with truth.

President Trump must govern over a divided house. Christ said a divided house cannot stand so, that tells where America is headed. The president will face many enemies, including his own mental mixture of good and evil knowledge. If he can maneuver a divided and self-centered congress, Supreme Court and citizenship into making decisions to help all the people, he will be on his way to success in restoring mental health but, the same strategy will not restore holy health. If he begins to succeed, Satan will use his most powerful weapon to defeat him. Satan's most powerful weapon is the one he used to defeat a god who had perfect intelligence and unlimited authority.

Because Adam was superior, Satan could not defeat him one-on-one but, he could defeat him with the help of Adam's greatest weakness. Like Adam, Mr. Trump's greatest challenge will come from a woman or a group of women. Some will admire him to the point of being willing to betray husbands and children to satisfy his desires. Some who hate him will use the same strategy to cause him dishonor. Some will persuade their feminized husbands to oppose him. God equipped women to rule the world by training children to do their bidding. This works for both good and evil. Because Eve usurped the authority of God, God placed her under the authority of man but, a woman doesn't need authority to defeat a man with authority.

Just as Eve rebelled against the authority of God, many women rebel against the authority of God by leaving the assignment God gave them. Because Eve refused to stay with the assignment God gave her to teach sons and daughters the words and ways of God, she set an example for all women. She was designed to be a succorer for her children and husband but her self-centered ambitions turned her away from the greatest assignment given to any human. The great number of women in places of influence makes America's chances of survival a long shot. If the lawyers don't pull his teeth, America's David will be defeated by one or more women.

As previously discussed, forty is a significant number. It represents something like an incubation period or the completion of time needed to be qualified to begin something. The election of the fortieth president began the last chapter of a once great America. Forty years later will be an election of a second term for Mr. Trump. If in his first four years America prospers, some converts will be won but America will not be healed. Using good knowledge, the people may reduce some of the conflict but they won't secure peace. The instructions God gave to Israel applies to America. Here are his instructions:

If my people who are called by my name: His name is not Jesus because this promise was made before the time of Jesus. His name is The Word of God. (Revelation 19:13). He is addressing people who believe what he says. This is a small percentage of the people of America who learn and trust the Word of God more than religion, government or theories of people who don't know God. Satan's people are not included.

Will humble themselves: (bend the knee): This is a denial of self and self-worth. It is an act of submission and humiliation.

Pray: This word means to judge. It is an honest and factual presentation of self to God.

Seek my face: Seek is to search until there is a face-face meeting with God. According to Christ, praying is done by an individual in a locked closet. Numbers only count when they are counted one-by-one. God is asking for individuals, not crowds, to seek an audience with him.

Turn from their wicked ways: These are people, called by his name, who are engaged in envy, strife, Jealousy, lying, anger, immorality, drunkenness, drugs, hatred, selfishness and things like these.

THEN

I will listen from Heaven: Even God can't solve America's problems using self-willed people.

I will forgive their sins: The word, forgive means to carry. Sin is an offence. It could mean an offence against self, others, God or all three. God said, the burdens which people called by his name have, he will carry for them. This promise was repeated by Christ. **Everyone who is exhausted and laboring under a load; come to me and I will rest you. Put my yoke on you and learn from me because I am gentle and humble in heart. You will find rest in your life because my yoke is well fitted and my load is light. (Matthew 11:28-30).**

I will heal their land: The only ointment that will heal the wounds of America is love. The only source of love is God. Israel kept adjusting the words of God until they were no longer people called by his name. With an empty hope they have spent 2,000 years waiting for their Messiah. America can spend the next 1,000 years with empty hope or, she can follow God's instructions and see him Make America Great Again. This is not a promise to a crowd at a religious meeting; this is a promise to individuals.

Satan will do everything he can to prevent this. The current president would be wise to remember the ability of Satan to make him angry at his opponents. Anger resides in the bosom of fools. A young man earning money as a sparring partner learned what follows anger. Be suspicious of women. The one that conquers may not realize she is being used by Satan. He used Eve and Sarah to persuade Adam and Abraham to ignore the instructions of God. He used Zipporah, the wife of Moses, to persuade Moses to ignore the instructions of God concerning circumcision. He used Delilah to defeat Samson and prevent Israel being freed from the bondage of the Philistines. He used Job's wife in a failed attempt to get Job to curse God because of the afflictions caused by Satan. He used Bathsheba to cause David to ignore God and commit adultery and murder. He used 1,000 women to feed Solomon's debauchery which led to the downfall of Israel.

There are many godly women but it should be remembered Eve, Sarah and Job's wife were godly women. Godly women and women who leave the assignment God gave them can be deceived by Satan and used to defeat men representing God. Satan knows the weaknesses of women and, as he did with Eve, he can use their beauty, intelligence and the delusion they are the "weaker sex" to persuade the president to disobey the instructions of God. The most powerful tool of Satan has always been a woman because she is the Achilles Heel of a man. A man who thinks he cannot be overcome by the charm of a woman is underestimating the ability of a woman coached by Satan.

A woman's fierce defense of her child carries over into a fierce defense of other possessions, including her ideas. She uses words to attack with her knowledge which generates heat in her opponent which increases the division. A self-confident man, facing an opponent, uses fewer and more tactful words because he believes he is stronger than his opponent. This keeps tempers at a lower temperature and provides a better opportunity for a solution to the disagreement. Men who are not feminized by a feminine environment, more closely resemble the way God designed them. They have an attitude similar to that of Theodore Roosevelt; "Speak softly but carry a big stick." No one questions a woman's intelligence. It is the way she uses her intelligence that disqualifies her for the assignment God gave man.

God made woman the most beautiful and most intelligent creature of all he made but, she is the prime example of great intelligence and beauty being destroyed by a desire for self. God gave her control of everything including man. The words of Mr. Wallace tell why. "The hand that rocks the cradle is the hand that rules the world." The woman has a relationship with the child that begins soon after inception. After it is born, she can mold that child into the image and likeness of God. When that child becomes an adult, it thinks and acts according to the mother's teachings. Its decisions are its mother's decisions. Satan knows, if he is to succeed in destroying man he must persuade women to abandon the assignment God gave them.

Because of her intelligence and appearance, commerce offers her fame and fortune. She becomes convinced as long as she is providing food, clothing, shelter and education for her child she is fulfilling her assignment. She depends upon the church to teach her child about God. Another person watches her child while she is fulfilling her desire. Her daughters and sons grow up being influenced more by peers and famous idols than her. The morality of a nation reveals how well women do the assignment God gave them. They hold the keys to the moral health of a nation. America will not return to the ways of God until women return to the assignment God gave them. This is not a realistic hope for America.

A woman, leaving the assignment God gave her to do man's work, is equivalent to a pilot of a large airplane filled with passengers, leaving the controls of the plane to help the stewardess serve snacks. Her reward is sons and daughters who grow up to represent

God; her penalty is sons and daughters who grow up to represent Satan. Not learning love and devotion from a mother, children become adults who don't know how to provide love and devotion to a mate or their children. The rejection of God's instructions produces a severe penalty for women. Many are abandoned by husbands not properly taught by a mother and must provide for her and her children or find another irresponsible man. In a society where mothers farm out their responsibility, anyone challenging what they are doing is faced with female anger. Mr. Wallace's words are worth quoting again; **"The hand that rocks the cradle is the hand that rules the world."** Good or bad; women are in control.

Observing the 6,000 year history of man gives some ideas of the way the world will look in the seventh millennial day.

1. Demons (gods) will continue to seduce people; creating thoughts which produce destructive results. Demons can affect the chemistry of the body to increase the force of a desire or distorted thinking. Medical science can see the chemistry causing the problem but, unless they understand the reality and strategy of demons, they will not discover what increases the force of chemistry to the limit of a person's ability to resist. A person saying, "I can't help myself", is not telling the truth. It is true, without the handicap of a physical body, demons are superior to humans. That's why God placed a limit on their ability comparable to the ability of the person they are trying to conquer. No one can say a stronger force overcame them. Their loss did not come from lack of ability but from lack of will to use their ability to defeat a demon offering them poisonous pleasure.

2. Women will continue to strive to do man's assignment instead of the one God assigned them. This will cause most of the children to adopt a religion or personal opinion that leaves them ignorant of God.

3. Religious systems will continue a façade of Godliness. Religion will be an opiate that will prevent people realizing they are not acceptable to God.

4. Religious differences, manifest as differences in opinions, will lead to many deaths and much destruction.
5. Imaginations of the human brain will become constantly evil like the people prior to the flood and cause nature to increase unleashing her forces against mankind. Floods, fires, storms, earthquakes, etc. will be common.
6. Ambition to be the best will generate an anything-goes attitude.
7. Laws will be used by leaders to rob, steal, dominate and kill citizens.
8. Socially accepted drugs will destroy immune systems, cause incurable diseases and be an open door for other drugs.
9. Commitment to one person in marriage will become out of reach because of the pre-marital practice of fornication. Children will be like puppies, deprived of learning the commitment of a man and woman in love, which represents a person and God being in love. This increases the difficulty of understanding the benefit of God's love.

Christ's statement concerning the Jews applies to the people of America. **These people honor me with words of their mouth but their hearts are kept far away from me. Teaching teachings that are precepts of men, they futilely attempt to worship me. (Matthew 15:8-9).**

Israel lived in their promised land about 300 years before they replaced God with a king. This king made Israel too weak to defend itself against its enemies. Finally, King Saul, wounded and facing defeat, committed suicide. God selected a man of courage and respect for God to replace King Saul. This was the beginning of the fourth millennial day. Israel prospered and became a wealthy and powerful nation. During the 1,000 years that followed, Israel had the Torah which contained God's instruction for successful living but the desires of the body and imaginations of the brain, manipulated by Satan, led them to defeat. When all else failed, God entered a human body in an effort to get Israel to return to truth. The audacity of God in Christ, questioning their religious beliefs made them angry. Using a mob to persuade Roman authority, they acquired permission to murder the physical body of God.

The seventh millennial day will be, for America, what the fourth millennial day was for Israel. Mr. Trump appears to be another David, selected by God to lead America to prosperity and power. She may again, be the envy of the world. However, because of her confidence in knowledge, God will only be a religious idea to most Americans, the way he was to Israel. The things that enable God to sustain her will not be trusted as much as wealth and what it can do. In time she will become an "also ran" like the other nations of the world. Laws of man, produced by expediency, will continue being the guide for thought and conduct which will give people of law more authority than God. Because laws are produced and function with knowledge, there will always be conflict.

Her churches will continue having a mixture of wheat and darnel without knowing which is which. She will become like other nations and no longer be respected as the land of the free and home of the brave. The people of the world will continue to be self-centered and blind to the reality of God. Then, at some moment, the last person to accept the love of God will physically die and make his way to Heaven. Then, without warning, God will delete time. This universe, like the scaffolding used to erect a building, will be set aside and nothing will remain except God, the redeemed and the non-human citizens of Heaven. If what Peter said is true, that's a little less than 1,000 years from the time of this writing.

It is evident mixed knowledge has been the root of the evil of this world. Because every human has a collection of mixed knowledge, the battle between faith and knowledge is a part of every person's life. A person must make certain he isn't deceived into thinking his good knowledge will make him acceptable to God. The Scribes and Pharisees had an abundance of good knowledge. A person's acceptance by God is not based upon his knowledge but upon his love for God; demonstrated by a love for fellow man. Love produces faith which causes a person to make what God says, preeminent over everything else. Here are some comparisons that might help in seeing the difference in faith and knowledge

1. Knowledge seeks to bring God down to man's level. Faith enables man to go to God's level.
2. Knowledge is the accumulation of learned information. Faith is not learned; it is the fruit of love.
3. Confidence is produced by compatible knowledge. Faith is produced by the spoken Word of God to a god living in a human body.
4. Knowledge is incomplete, changed by new knowledge and subject to becoming obsolete. Faith is complete, consistent with new faith and always current.
5. Knowledge is energized by desire for personal gain. Faith is energized by love for God, manifest by a love for others.
6. Knowledge requires time for results. Faith is instant.
7. Knowledge is temporal. Faith has no end.
8. Knowledge requires proof. Faith is proof.

Faith is the existence of that for which we hope. It is proof of an unseen, accomplished fact. (Hebrews 11:1)

THE END OF THE SEVENTH
MILLENNIAL DAY

At the end of millennial day seven, when time is deleted, Satan and the last of those he deceived will be destroyed. All of the first creation will cease to exist and nothing will be left except God, his heavenly servants and those who accepted his love. God will provide a new heaven and earth where there will not be a body filled with desire or a brain filled with mixed knowledge. The greatest human dream will be reality.

The total project is clearly explained in the Old Testament and the words of Christ. God is searching for someone to love him the way he loves them. Satan, like a jealous and rejected suitor, is determined this will not happen. The life in the kernel of corn planted in the soil attracts all life in the soil but, only that life willing to leave the soil, not be content with being a part of the plant (religious) but totally committing to become a kernel, is harvested. For a human, only love will produce total commitment. It is important not to confuse like with love or hope with faith.

A person can completely commit and be a part of God's kind of life or remain a part of the life of this world. God gives him the freedom to choose. This world has many wonderful things to offer. Enjoying them without being possessed by them is what God intended. Liking them to the point of making them more important than God is what causes the problem. The problem with making them first in life is; they only satisfy the body and its brain which eventually die and leave the god who lived in the body without anything.

When a man loves a woman who loves him, the primary purpose of life for both is complete. Contentment closes the door on every other attraction and everything that touches them. There is nothing that can diminish their love for each other. Enduring together the worst of living conditions, makes the love of two people stronger and more beautiful. The most beautiful face is the face of the person loved. Some of the most beautiful roses are those growing out of a dung hill. All God ever wanted was someone like him, who would love him the way he loves them. God, like humans, does not want a mate who does not make him the most important thing in their life. Love is born with absolute freedom to choose. It cannot be produced with a promise of Heaven or a threat of *hell.*

The twentieth chapter of Revelation reveals what has been happening since the death of Christ. The end of the seventh millennial day will be the end of this activity in God's Supreme Court.

There are many ideas concerning what this information means. As previously discussed, Gethsemane and the crucifixion was the greatest of all great days of God. That was when Christ defeated the power of his brain which Adam did not do. To understand Revelation, the symbols must be understood. Here are some of the symbols found in Revelation 20. The KJV is in parenthesis.

Abyss-(bottomless pit)-abussou is a boundless area. The only thing in time that is without bounds is the human brain. It can receive information from God and Satan who are beyond the realm of time. This is seen in the messenger from heaven, who has the key that permits him to enter the brain (abyss).

Great chain-The word "alusis" (chain) is a way of binding something. Satan is not physical so he cannot be bound with a physical chain; he can only be bound with the words of God. He is like a dog on a lease that is limited in what he can do. Paul understood this when he said, **"None but human trials take hold of you. God, who is faithful, will not allow you to be tried beyond your ability but, will provide, with the trial, ability to move from under it. (I Corinthians 10:13).**

He bound him 1,000 years-1,000 (Hebrew-elef) represents commonality such as time, family, race, cause, the time a person lives, etc. Satan and his demons, like humans, have different personalities. They are bound to different people during the lifetime of the people. The more demons a person has, the less he has control of his brain. Demons use different body fluids that affect human behavior. A psychiatrist whose patient was cured by exorcism was permitted to listen to a recording of the voices of the demons speaking from his patient during the exorcism. He said he was preparing a paper that dealt with this kind of "phenomena". The minister asked him if he would, like Christ, call the cause of his patient's problems, demons. He exclaimed, "No! I would be laughed out of the AMA". Are these not the people trusted by most people? Who knows more about human problems; medical people or Christ?

When the unclean breath (demon) is cast out of a man, he travels through waterless places seeking rest and finds none. Finally he says, "I will return to my house which I left." Upon arrival he finds it unoccupied, cleanly swept and arranged in an orderly manner. He then goes and takes with him seven different kinds of breaths, more evil than he, and entering, makes that his dwelling. The latter condition of that man becomes worse than he was before. This is the way it is with this evil generation. (Matthew 12:43-45). Christ is speaking of a person who overcame a problem and cleaned up his life but, didn't invite God to be a co-tenant with him. His life was clean but empty. He lived an exemplary life for a time but, a clean life without God in it is like a clean, empty house. Eventually, losers will occupy it. A human brain, not occupied by God, will eventually become an abode for demons. At the end of a person's life (1,000), his demons are set free for a short time until Satan assigns them to another person willing to listen to them.

Lived and reigned with Christ 1,000 years-This is the message Christ told the seventy to tell the people. These are redeemed gods, living in human bodies, who are revived when they accept God's love. These people live the remainder of their physical lives (1,000), reigning with God on earth. The rest of the dead (the unsaved) do not live until the end of their lives (1,000) when they are revived to represent themselves at their judgment. All ignorance is removed and they stand before God with a clear understanding of their situation.

Gog and Magog-Gog was a son of Shemarah, a prophet during the time of Rehoboam, Solomon's son. Magog was a son of Japheth, one of the three sons of Noah. The tribes of Israel separated during the reign of Rehoboam. In Ezekiel 38 & 39, Gog is seen as the object of the wrath of God. Magog is also referred to as a country. It was common for Christ to compare current situations with past events and people.

Books and book-The Greek word allo identifies the books to be the same kind as the book. Biblia, from which came the word bible, is the word translated book and books. Both, the book and the books, contain the words of God which act as an advocate for the believer and an adversary for the unbeliever. A person in court, facing a judge, is not judged by the judge but by what is written in the books of law. The same law that rules one person guilty, rules another person not guilty. At this judgment, a person's guilt or innocence is determined by that which is written in the books. Those revived by love which produced faith are in the book of life. Christ said it would not be him but his words that would be the judge. (John 12:47-48).

Book of life-Those who accept the love of God, as demonstrated in Christ, have no charge brought against them at final judgment. Those who represent themselves are proven guilty by their earthly conduct and sentenced to die in the Lake of Fire. There is a popular saying of lawyers: "A person who represents himself in a court of law has a fool for a lawyer." This is especially true for the person who stands in God's supreme court of justice representing himself.

Lake of fire- This corresponds to the times Christ told of the grain being harvested and the stalks being burned. Both stalk and grain are produced by the same seed but only that commitment which surpasses the level of the stalk to become a duplicate of the seed is harvested. The stalk represents religious people whose allegiance is to a religious order instead of God. Satan, the religious systems which replaced God with rules and teachings, the religious and other teachers who misrepresented God, death (man's worst enemy) and ignorance, (Satan's most powerful tool), will all meet their end in the Lake of Fire.

The lake of fire is not a place of punishment. This misunderstanding was caused by translators taking the descriptions of gehenna and hades and applying them to the made-up word hell to protect a tradition. As previously mentioned, gehenna and hades describe conditions in the lifetime of some people. The lake of fire is a place of extermination. God's purpose for creating man was to have someone like him to share his love. If a man offers his love to a woman and she declines his offer, he doesn't harm her, he leaves her alone. It is the same with God.

There is only one of two places a person can go when he leaves his body. One is Heaven and the other is the lake of fire. God offers his love to each person while he is alive in his physical body. That is the only time a person can accept God's offer of love. Trying to understand why the insects, mentioned at the beginning of the book, kept moving toward the fire until it killed them is like trying to understand why people keep moving toward the lake of fire until it finally kills them. There is more than enough warning for the insects and people, but something causes them to continue until they die. Neither God nor other people are responsible for this obsession with something that destroys life. The penalty for the unsaved is not punishment; it is missing life with God and others in a paradise void of any pain or sadness.

In 20:10 the statement "tormented day and night forever and ever" needs a close look. Day and night are periods of time. There is no day and night or time in the nonphysical world so these words represent something that occurred in the lifetime of a person. The same is true of the words "forever and forever". A day and night represents one day. As previously shown, the Greek word aion represents life as in life span and ainios represents forever or without end. Both of the words used here are aion.

The Greek word "basanisthasontai" (torment-KJV) means to test with a touchstone. A touchstone is a hard stone used to test the quality of gold and silver. The word is in past tense which means the test was applied in the past to the people in question. These were people who represented Satan with their speech and conduct. What they thought was their conscious was the touchstone of truth testing them concerning their acceptability to God. The words in 20:9: "fire came down out of heaven and devoured them" are words added by a scribe. They are not in the accepted manuscripts.

The deceiver (devil) representing Satan was another human. That deceiver was being tested day and night throughout the days of his life, by the touchstone of truth to see if what he believed was real or fake. Every day of his life he was faced with truth about himself. He is in the same category as the religious person and the false religious leader. A voice is always telling him he is wrong but he refuses to heed the voice. His destiny is to be thrown into the Lake of fire of the divine. Theios (brimstone) means divine. In exorcisms, when a minister puts his hand upon the forehead of a person possessed of demons, that person may feel heat much higher than body temperature. A person being closely questioned who is lying is said to be on the "hot seat". People committed to evil don't like being in the presence of people who represent God. Truth is a touchstone that challenges people to see if they are genuine or fake.

The deceiving person, deceiving them, was thrown into the Lake of divine fire where the small wild animal and false leaders are. They had been put to the test, day and night, every day of their lives. I saw a large white throne. The heaven and earth fled from the presence of the one sitting upon it and there was no place found for them. I saw the dead; the insignificant and the famous; standing before the throne. Books were opened and, another book like them was opened, which is the Book of Life. The dead were judged by their conduct, according to that which had been written in the books. The sea gave the dead in her and death and ignorance (hades), gave the dead in them and each of them was judged according to their conduct. Death, and ignorance, was thrown into the Lake of Fire. The Lake of Fire is the second death. If someone was not recorded in the Book of Life, he was thrown into the Lake of Fire. (Revelation 20:10-15).

To make sure no religious person assumes something not true, Christ said, **Not all who are saying to me, "Lord, Lord, will enter into the reign of God. It will be those doing the will of my father** in the heavens. Many will say to me in that day, Lord; Lord; did we not preach, and with your name cast out demons and with the power of your name do many things. I will agree with them and then tell them, "I never knew you."

The dead come from three areas.

1. The sea- In 17:15, sea represents people. These are people killed by people.
2. Death-these died from natural causes.
3. Ignorance (haides)- these were the foolish who killed themselves with alcohol, tobacco, other drugs, food etc.

Then, for the total population, the people not overcoming the challenges of this world are among the condemned.

The timid-These are people too afraid to take a stand for truth in the face of opposition.

Faithless-These are people who did not experience love which produces faith

The filthy-These are people with vile language and sordid conduct.

Murderers-This is killing because of anger, hatred or for benefit.

Male prostitutes- The word used here is masculine but represents both male and female. These are men and women who engage in sex for hire.

Drug users and providers-This Greek word is pharmakos (pharmacy). There is no evidence to prove differently so, the reader will have to determine if this this includes drugs needed to maintain health.

Idolators-These are people who worship other people, images and objects in violation of God's instruction to have no other objects of worship.

All liars-Truth represents God and a lie represents Satan. Saying a person who lies is possessed by Satan is not a criticism; it is a statement of fact. Christ said Satan is the father of liars.

Instead of having a place in Heaven, all of the people in the groups listed above will have their place in the lake that is burning with divine fire. (brimstone-divine=theio). **The timid, faithless, abominable, murderers, prostitutes, drug users, idolaters and all liars will have their place in the lake burning with divine fire which is the second death. (Revelation21:8).** The insects died before they could reach the fire. The three Hebrew men were immune to the fire because God was in the fire with them. Life is not a movie where those who die appear in a later movie. Life is reality. Not everyone can know the correct information but, everyone has the capacity to love. Love cannot be produced or controlled by circumstances or religious teachings. Everyone has the freedom to love. God offers his love to everyone.

The influence of those in heaven and those on earth cannot influence this hearing at God's Supreme Court. This destroys the idea prayers can be made for someone who died or praying to someone like Mary or some saint can be an influence at this hearing. The only witness for a person whose name is not recorded in the Book of Life is what he was while he lived in his body. He is his only character witness.

Status, wealth and power in physical life have no influence in this court. Lady Justice still wears her blindfold in this court. The great ones don't get special treatment and the poor don't get pity. The book and the books are the same kind of books. There is only one code used to determine the outcome. That code is the words spoken by God. Christ told the people he would not judge them but his words would. It is the words of Christ that deem a person innocent or guilty.

Most people don't know laws but many naturally, live a life in agreement with laws because love is their standard for living. It is not necessary to know what Christ said for the person living a life in agreement with what Christ said. Those whose names are recorded in the Book of Life are not dead because the words of Christ revived them when they accepted and returned his love. It is love of God, not knowledge of God that makes a person acceptable to God. People not loving are temporarily revived to stand trial. Otherwise, the Lake of Fire would not be a second death for them.

In millennial day seven God will pause. The people of the world will be on their own to make their choices. His proposal of love will remain open to the last second of time. Then he will clean the premises by deleting time and, this creation, like the scaffolding used to build a building, will be taken away.

Conclusion

God created this world and universe in an effort to find someone like him who would love him as he loves them. Loves requires complete freedom to choose. For that reason, one of Satan's prime goals is to confuse the meaning of love. The human brain can use circumstances and thoughts to produce a "like" for something or someone but it can't produce love. That is reserved for the god living in the body. If the god in the human body does not experience love, he does not experience God. People say they love cars, houses, clothes, etc. They don't love these things; they like these things. A person may like someone they don't love and love someone they don't like.

The Greek language makes a distinction for the word love. Eros is desire produced by the appetites of the body. This isn't love, it is physical desire. Phileo represents thoughts produced by the brain. This is mental friendship and is expressed by liking something or someone. It is reciprocal or a two way relationship which can be ended if like changes to dislike. Agape is the only word that represents love. This originates with God and is granted to a god in a human body that will return it to God. It is not produced; it is a gift from God. It is not controlled; there is no limit to what a person of love will do or forgive. It cannot be destroyed. The pain of rejected love is the greatest of pains. A person with this pain would gladly destroy it if he could. It caused Christ to weep because the people of Jerusalem rejected him. Note the three middle letters in Jer USA lem.

Paul had some theological errors, as all people do but, he listed characteristics of agape love (KJV-charity) that agree with Christ and what he said about love. **If I am speaking with the human tongue of a heavenly messenger but, I don't have love; I am like** the sound of brass coins or repetitious cymbals. If I am able to prophesy, know every mystery, have all knowledge and, have the faith needed to move a mountain from place to place but, I don't have love; I am nothing. If since I began (born), I gave every crumb of food; even if I should give my body to be burned but, I don't have love, there is no benefit for me.

Love does not lose heart; love is mild. Love is not zealous; not boastful; not carnally natural; not unbelieving; does not seek for itself; does not irritate; does not reason with evil; is not glad for something unrighteous but is glad for truth. It is always protecting; always believing; always hoping; always bearing up under the load. Love never falls down. –Paul-I Corinthians 13:1-8a).

There are many wonderful people in this world who do wonderful things. It is tragic so many fall prey to the evil knowledge of Satan and miss the saving power of love.

I saw a new heaven and a new earth. The first heaven and earth no longer existed and there were no longer, people (sea). I saw the holy city, New Jerusalem, descended from God out of heaven, made ready like a bride adorned by her husband. (Revelation 21:1-2). This is what a person who loves God can see. Sea represents people-17:15. The fact John was looking at this proves it existed at that time. It doesn't wait until the end of time to exist.

An octave in music consists of eight notes. The eighth note is a reproduction of the first note on a higher scale. Just as the eighth original day was the beginning of a relationship between God and man in a new world, so it will be on the eighth timeless day when God will share all he is and has with those who accepted his love. Life in the New Heaven and Earth will be similar to life in the current heaven and earth but the absence of a physical body will enable the love that began on earth to reign supreme in the new heaven and earth. Instead of depending upon a brain to process knowledge, citizens of this new world will be aware of everything. There won't be a need for fig leaves because no one will have anything to hide.

HEAVEN

I heard that Heaven is a very wealthy place.
It has gates of pearl which are hinged on grace.
Pure water in the river supplies all the land
and twelve kinds of fruit are picked by hand.
Gold is used for paving; that must be a sight.
Precious gems glitter, reflecting Heaven's light.
Light is always shining, but not from the sun.
Night is gone forever; not seen by anyone.
There are no tears there to dampen the face.
Tears were dried by God's loving embrace.
There is no pain there from sickness or sorrow
and no stress for what might come tomorrow.
Meadows extend forever inviting a stroll.
The sky is dressed with beauty inspiring the soul.
Laughter sounds like music floating on the air.
Kindness, like a spring, is flowing everywhere.
No one is giving orders; no one to obey
because Christ, as a brother, is showing the way.
No one is bigger...no one better than me
because everyone is family. We all agree.
This place is home to all the redeemed.
It is not something some human schemed.
In whom all things exist, whatever existence is,
was nailed to a cross; not my cross but his.
Yet, the many wonders of this wondrous place
will not seem like Heaven until I see your face.
The greatest of all treasures cannot please my soul
until shared with loved ones who make me whole.
Like the love of God, in my life I have found
love sets one free but it also keeps him bound.
Without the people I love, Heaven will be bare.
Heaven is not Heaven without loved ones to share.
What are you expecting when you enter Heaven's door?
Will Heaven be sufficient or will you ask for more?

Will those you love greet you as you walk through the gate?
Then Heaven will be Heaven and your joy will be great.
To help secure these treasures while living here on earth,
give your love to God and love for all you're worth.
Tell each and every loved one how empty Heaven will be
if you look at all the faces and their face you do not see.

Best wishes to you and yours,
Kris Doulos

Printed in the United States
By Bookmasters